essential resources

SOLO Taxonomy and English Language Learners

Making second language learning visible

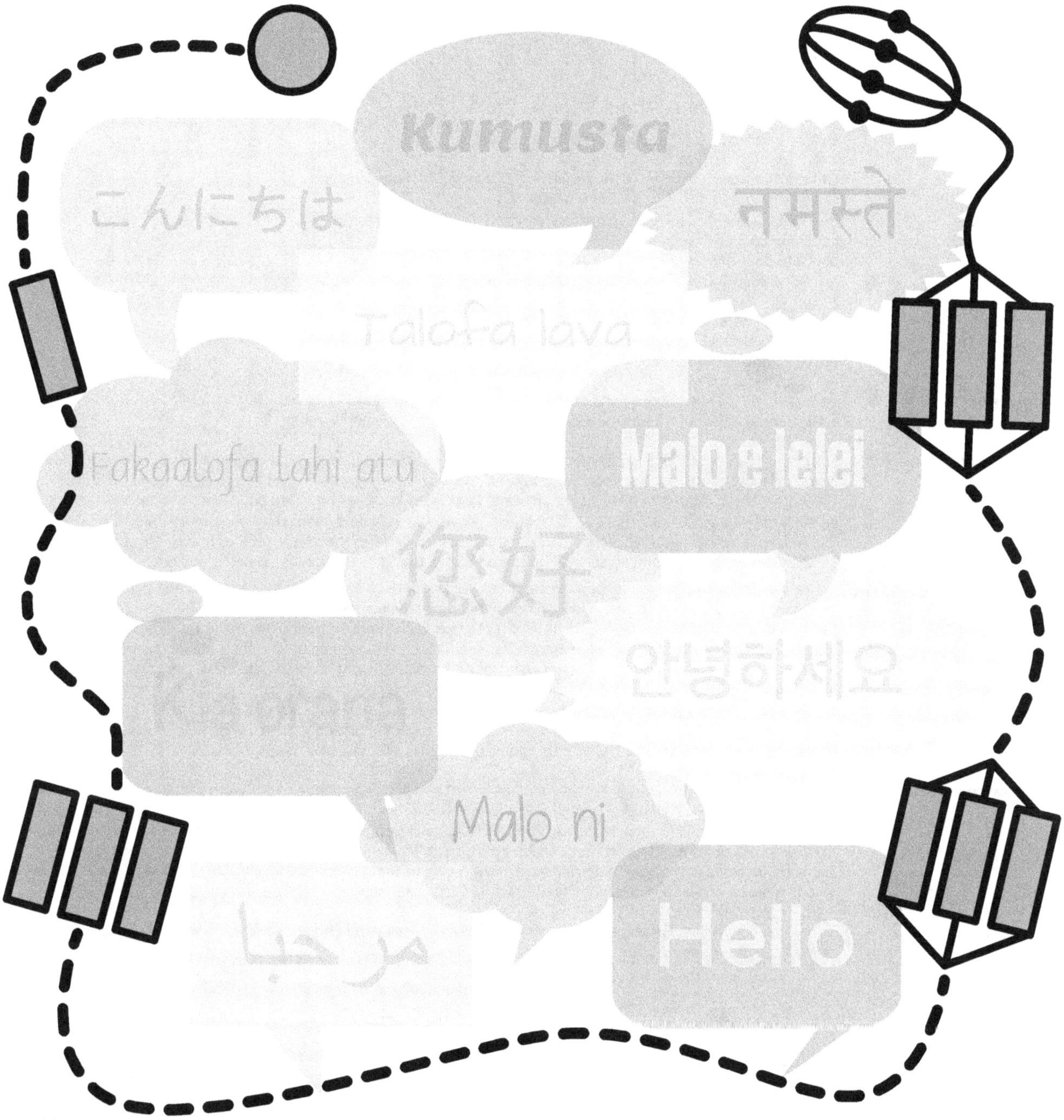

Pam Hook and Sonya Van Schaijik

Title:	SOLO Taxonomy and English Language Learners Making second language learning visible
Authors:	Pam Hook and Sonya Van Schaijik
Editor:	Tanya Tremewan
Designer:	Diane Williams
Book code:	5937
ISBN:	978-1-77655-226-9
Published:	2016
Publisher:	Essential Resources Educational Publishers Limited

United Kingdom:	Australia:	New Zealand:
Units 8–10 Parkside	PO Box 906	PO Box 5036
Shortgate Lane	Strawberry Hills	Invercargill
Laughton BN8 6DG	NSW 2012	
ph: 0845 3636 147	ph: 1800 005 068	ph: 0800 087 376
fax: 0845 3636 148	fax: 1800 981 213	fax: 0800 937 825

Websites: www.essentialresourcesuk.com
www.essentialresources.com.au
www.essentialresources.co.nz

Copyright: Text: © Pam Hook and Sonya Van Schaijik, 2016
Edition and illustrations: © Essential Resources Educational Publishers Limited, 2016

About the authors: Pam Hook is an educational consultant (HookED Educational Consultancy, www.pamhook.com), who works with New Zealand and Australian schools to develop curricula and pedagogies for learning to learn based on SOLO Taxonomy. She has published articles on thinking, learning, e-learning and gifted education, and has written curriculum material for government and business. As well as authoring and co-authoring more than 15 books on SOLO Taxonomy (some of which have been translated into Danish), she is co-author of two science textbooks widely used in New Zealand secondary schools. She is also a popular keynote speaker at conferences.

Sonya Van Schaijik is an experienced teacher from Auckland, New Zealand, whose teaching and thinking are underpinned by SOLO Taxonomy and recorded in her blog (www.sonyavanschaijik.com). She is tattooed with the Samoan woman's malu, is a bilingual learner who speaks Samoan fluently, and has trained in effective pedagogies for bilingual education and ESOL. At Newmarket Primary School, she has responsibility for the integration of technology into teaching and learning programmes in ways that maximise student learning outcomes. Her considerable experience in building and leading e-learning communities for teachers and students includes introducing and coordinating TeachMeetNZ, which promotes conversations on effective pedagogies (including ESOL), being actively involved in the Flat Connections Global Project and leading groups of teachers on Connected Educator. She was a recipient of an e-fellowship with CORE Education Ltd in 2011 and TeachNZ fellowship in 2013.

Acknowledgements: Thanks to Professor John Biggs for his encouragement and ongoing critique of our work with the classroom-based approach to using SOLO Taxonomy, and to the many New Zealand schools who have shared SOLO as a common language of learning with their students. Special thanks to principal Dr Wendy Kofoed, staff, parents and children from Newmarket Primary School (Auckland, New Zealand) for the many examples of English language learners' learning outcomes in the book. Special thanks also to Virginia Kung (Deputy Principal, Newmarket Primary School), who continually challenges pedagogy framed with SOLO Taxonomy.

Dedication: To my parents, Ronald Frederick Reynolds and Kathleen Therese née Thompson. This book is dedicated to you with all my heart; it is because of you that I am bilingual. *Sonya Van Schaijik*

Copyright notice:

All rights reserved. No part of this publication may be reproduced, stored in a retrieval system, or transmitted in any form by any means, electronic or mechanical or by photocopying, recording or otherwise, without the prior written permission of the publisher. Copyright owners may take legal action against a person or organisation who infringes their copyright through unauthorised copying. All inquiries should be directed to the publisher at the address above.

Contents

Introduction	**4**
1. An overview of SOLO Taxonomy and effective pedagogies for English language learners	**6**
What is SOLO Taxonomy?	6
What is effective pedagogy for ELLs?	8
2. What SOLO can do for L2 acquisition and next steps	**10**
Stages in language acquisition	10
Stages in cognitive complexity of task and outcome	11
Strategies for planning the order and sequence of language acquisition experiences	17
3. Building academic L2	**24**
General approaches and strategies	24
SOLO-based approaches and strategies	28
4. Text patterns for academic English	**44**
Text patterns for bringing in ideas (multistructural tasks)	44
Text patterns for connecting ideas (relational task)	50
Text patterns for extending ideas (extended abstract task)	62
Conclusions	**68**
References	**69**
Index of figures, tables and exhibits	**70**

Introduction

*As I have observed in very many classrooms over the years I have decided that what is needed above knowledge, teaching skills, cultural awareness and personal qualities like enthusiasm is **the idea of balance**.* (Brown 2011, p 67)

The idea of balance is central to teachers of English as a second language (L2). Brown (2011), who has seen many different second language pedagogies and practices espoused and enacted over the years of her scholarship and teaching, argues that "balance" in teaching is a critical component in the lasting success of L2 acquisition. This includes the balance between:

> accepting silence versus encouraging talk; language focus based on pre-determined needs versus language focus based on students' immediate needs; modelling and scaffolding versus student creativity; correcting versus not correcting; old work versus new work; learning L2 versus encouraging L1 [first language]; and culturally relevant input versus exposure to new culture. (Brown 2011)

Figure 1 summarises these different components in achieving balance.

Figure 1: Components to balance in teaching English as a second language

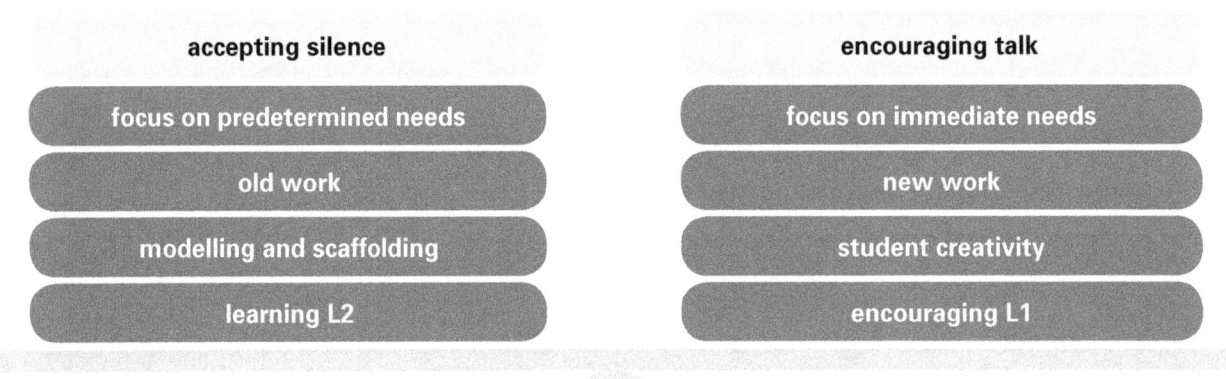

Source: Based on Brown (2011)

In *SOLO Taxonomy and English Language Learners*, we share ways in which we have used SOLO Taxonomy to support our search for balance when teaching English language learners (ELLs). Providing such balance is important work and getting it right is an ongoing challenge (Brown 2011, p 68).

Academic language: a key to successful learning

Academic language is "the language used in schools to help students acquire and use knowledge" (Anstrom et al 2010, cited in Schleppegrell 2012). Learning in school requires that all students, including ELLs, can use academic language and cognitively challenging processes to relate and extend ideas in abstract ways. Balancing opportunities to bring in the ideas and information (surface learning) with opportunities for connection and abstraction (deep learning) is made easier using SOLO Taxonomy.

All students need academic language to achieve in school. Academic language is much harder (and takes longer) to acquire when instruction is in a second language. If we do not actively seek explicit opportunities for ELLs to develop this academic language, we risk locking them into a pattern of long-term underachievement. Without key academic vocabulary (high-utility words) and text patterns, they are unlikely to develop the skills needed for academic success. It is the variable access to academic language – the "language of school" – that makes the teaching of academic registers to students an equity issue:

> Teaching students academic registers is an equity issue, as some children gain access to these registers outside of school through family and community activities, while other students need support in the classroom if they are to learn to engage in using language in ways that enable them to demonstrate their knowledge. (Schleppegrell 2012, p 412)

An overview of Newmarket Primary School, Auckland, New Zealand
Much of the experience and practical examples reported in this book come from Newmarket Primary School. Our students bring over 32 different languages to the school. Under a third of our students are funded for English for speakers of other languages (ESOL). Of these students, over half are from migrant families and the rest are New Zealand born. Like many inner city Auckland schools, our demographics are changing. In 2007 our roll was 43% Asian, 39% Pākehā (New Zealand European) and 5% Māori. Eight years later in 2015, the percentage of Māori remained the same but the proportion of Asians had increased to 62%. Our biggest ethnic group was Chinese at 28% of our roll, nearly double the 2007 figure.

In our experience, teachers must proactively seek **explicit** opportunities for teaching academic structures in L2 learning. Many classroom teachers will tell you that immersing ELLs in the everyday richness and collaboration in a student-centred English medium classroom is effective in developing L2 conversational fluency. They will report that after six to twelve months in an English medium school, many ELLs have acquired conversational fluency in English: they "fit right in", "have made great friends" and "have no problems interacting socially in class". This outcome is pleasing and seems to validate teaching practice but it can lead teachers to neglect balance – to overlook underachievement in academic contexts and to believe that these students no longer need explicit language learning support. This happens when **conversational fluency masks the lack of any academic language proficiency** – and this is important because academic language is necessary for future achievement and academic success (Gu 2013).

Indeed, the first time many teachers identify a need for any explicit teaching of academic language (academic vocabulary and grammar) is when achievement data drop across Year 3 as learning tasks become more challenging. In Year 3, reading comprehension replaces simpler decoding tasks and explanation-style writing replaces description.

Cummins (1979) explains that conversational fluency (Basic Interpersonal Communicative Skills, BICS) is cognitively undemanding and easy to acquire relative to academic language (Cognitive Academic Language Proficiency, CALP). ELLs take from five to seven years to acquire academic language, much longer than the conversational fluency so readily acquired in the first six to twelve months of joining a class. Classroom teachers need explicit pedagogical content knowledge to help all students develop proficiency in academic language structures and outcomes.

Additive language learning and providing opportunities for academic language learning

In our programmes, and in all our conversations with parents, we encourage balance through **additive language learning** – that is, the ongoing use and development of L1 when learning L2. Like May (2002), Cook (2005) and Macaro (2005), we believe that development of L1 produces a number of important advantages for L2 learning. May (2002) claims further that "The least effective way of teaching a majority language (English, in our context) is by problematising and/or excluding first languages". Using and encouraging the use of L1 recognises individual learners so that they feel like they belong. Indeed, Edstrom (2006, cited in Ellis and Shintani 2013, p 230) states that teachers have **a moral obligation to communicate respect** to individual students in their classrooms. In addition, additive language learning helps ensure active schema exist in L1 for academic language acquisition in the L2 (Cummins 1994).

The balance between L1 and L2 helps when building personal relationships with students and their families and reducing anxiety in the classroom and anxiety about what might be happening in the classroom – high trust tasks often requiring conversational skills that lie outside those available in L2. Furthermore, a recent report from the Education Review Office (ERO) identifies that student success and achievement are accelerated when learning at home is actively promoted within the parent–teacher relationship (ERO 2015). Going further is the argument that the alternative – "subtractive learning of dominant languages – may **violate linguistic human rights and contribute to linguistic genocide**" (Skutnabb-Kangas and Phillipson 2008).

It is our experience that integrating SOLO Taxonomy and additive language approaches increases the likelihood that children's schema for academic language and higher-order thinking are acquired in the L2. We create explicit opportunities for academic L2 learning by fully integrating SOLO with L2 input and output in ways that balance listening, speaking, reading and writing. We find that SOLO is effective in developing active schema for conceptual or higher-order understandings across L1 and L2 contexts. SOLO is a common language for learning (Hook 2015).

1. An overview of SOLO Taxonomy and effective pedagogies for English language learners

O le tama a le manu e fafaga i ia ma fuga o laau, ao le tama a le tagata e fafaga i upu ma tala.

Animals and birds feed their young with fish and blooms or berries of trees but the young of humans shall be fed with words. Samoan proverb (Le Tagaloa 1996, p 16)

What is SOLO Taxonomy?

Structure of the Observed Learning Outcome (SOLO) Taxonomy is a model of learning. The model represents the ascending structural complexity of learning outcomes as learning progresses through surface, deep and conceptual levels of understanding.

The model describes five distinct levels of learning outcome: learning outcomes that show no idea (prestructural), one idea (unistructural), several ideas (multistructural), related ideas (relational) and extended ideas (extended abstract). These levels can be communicated through terms, symbols, hand signs and academic verbs (Table 1.1).

Table 1.1: SOLO levels, symbols, hand signs and academic verbs

Prestructural	Unistructural	Multistructural	Relational	Extended abstract
No idea	*One idea*	*Many loose ideas*	*Related ideas*	*Extended ideas*
Learning outcomes show unconnected information, no organisation.	Learning outcomes show simple connections but importance not noted.	Learning outcomes show connections are made, but significance to overall meaning is missing.	Learning outcomes show full connections made, and synthesis of parts to the overall meaning.	Learning outcomes go beyond subject and makes links to other concepts – generalises, predicts, evaluates.
	define, name, label, identify	describe, list, elaborate	sequence, classify, compare and contrast, explain causes, explain effects, analyse	generalise, predict, evaluate, create

As learning progresses, the SOLO levels represent two changes in the learning outcome:
- a **quantitative** increase in understanding (bringing in ideas – knowing more, moving from unistructural to multistructural outcomes)
- a **qualitative** change in understanding (linking ideas and extending ideas – deepening of understanding when moving from multistructural to relational to extended abstract outcomes) (Biggs and Tang 2007).

Students and teachers can use the model to describe the cognitive complexity of a learning outcome and how learning outcomes change and become more complex as any academic task is mastered (Biggs 1999). In this way, SOLO makes visible:

- the **structure** of learning – what is the structure of the ideas – are they loose, connected or extended ideas?
- the **process** of learning – what is the process when learning one idea or many ideas, relating ideas and extending ideas?

SOLO Taxonomy is an evidence-based model developed by university academics Biggs and Collis in the late 1970s. Their evidence came from research on the structure of samples of student thinking in many different subjects (and across many different levels).

When using SOLO, the focus is on the complexity of the structure of the student response, rather than on a categorisation of the student himself or herself. In this way, the model allows us to focus on "what the student does" rather than "what the student is" or "what the teacher does" (Biggs and Tang 2007, p 16). SOLO enables differentiation by outcome.

SOLO can be used to look at **declarative knowledge** (knowing about …) and **functioning knowledge** (knowing how to …).

Functioning knowledge (knowing how to)

The different levels of functioning knowledge outcomes are evident:

- when students are asked to apply their understanding; for example, when responding to pre and early production questions by pointing, drawing or responding with one word, or engaging in reciprocal teaching interactions with others
- through competencies and capabilities for living and learning with others; for example, when students are reflecting, managing self, using the senses to create mental pictures, participating and collaborating with others or choosing the best graphic organisers to help plan their ideas.

Table 1.2 presents a self-assessment rubric students can use to identify the SOLO level of their functioning knowledge.

Table 1.2: Self-assessment rubric for functioning knowledge, built using levels in SOLO Taxonomy

Functioning knowledge – knowing how to	Prestructural	Unistructural	Multistructural	Relational	Extended abstract
	Needs help	If directed	Aware but no reasons, has a go, makes mistakes	Purposeful, strategic, knows why and when, can identify mistakes	New ways, seeks feedback to improve, acts as role model, teaches others
Learning intention [verb] [content] [context]	I need help to start.	I can [xxxx] if directed or shown exactly what to do.	I can [xxxx] but I don't know why or when so it is trial and error. I make mistakes.	I can [xxxx] and I know why and when. I am strategic or purposeful and can find and correct my own mistakes …	… **and** I seek feedback to improve, help others and am a role model for them, and I find new ways of doing [xxxx].

Note: For the HookED SOLO Functioning Knowledge Rubric Generator, go to: http://pamhook.com/solo-apps/functioning-knowledge-rubric-generator

Declarative knowledge (knowing about)

Using SOLO, declarative knowledge is differentiated into what students can write about or talk about in different contexts. It is evident when students are asked to describe what they know about a particular topic, character or theme – for example, a person, place, thing or event.

Table 1.3 presents a self-assessment rubric students can use to identify the SOLO level of their declarative knowledge.

Table 1.3: Self-assessment rubric for declarative knowledge, built using levels in SOLO Taxonomy

Declarative knowledge – knowing about	Prestructural Needs help	Unistructural One relevant idea	Multistructural Several relevant ideas	Relational Linked ideas	Extended abstract Extended ideas
Learning intention [verb] [content] [context]	I need help to start.	My [learning outcome] has one relevant idea.	My [learning outcome] has several relevant ideas …	… **and** links these ideas (eg, *sequence, classify, compare and contrast, explain causes or effects, analyse part–whole*) …	… **and** looks at them in a new way (eg, *generalise, evaluate, predict, create*).

Note: For the HookED SOLO Declarative Knowledge Rubric Generator, go to: http://pamhook.com/solo-apps/declarative-knowledge-rubric-generator

What is effective pedagogy for ELLs?

Ellis and Shintani (2013, pp 22–27) identify a set of 11 general principles that inform instructed language learning, as well as giving procedural examples for implementation by teachers. These provide a useful framework for teachers designing effective teaching and learning experiences for ELLs. Exhibit 1.1 reframes them as check box questions, which can prompt you in planning for academic achievement in L2 learning (see also the SOLO L2 planning framework in Section 3). Each point represents an approach ensuring we are "feeding the young with words" (as in the Samoan proverb at the start of this section).

Exhibit 1.1: Checklist of questions when planning for academic achievement in L2 learning

☐	1. Does instruction develop **formulaic expressions** and a **rule-based** competence?	☐	7. Does instruction provide **opportunities to output**?
☐	2. Does instruction ensure learners focus on **meaning**?	☐	8. Does instruction emphasise **opportunity to interact in the L2**?
☐	3. Does instruction include a focus on **form**?	☐	9. Does instruction plan for **individual differences in learning**?
☐	4. Does instruction develop **implicit knowledge** and **explicit knowledge**?	☐	10. Does instruction **allow for subjectivity**?
☐	5. Does instruction reference the **order and sequence of L2 acquisition**?	☐	11. Does assessment examine **free** and **controlled** production?
☐	6. Does instruction ensure extensive **L2 input**?		

Source: Based on Ellis and Shintani (2013)

To be effective, the principles for L2 learning must align with our current understandings of how learners learn (Ellis and Shintani 2013). This suggests L2 teachers should also provide:

- **clear learning outcomes** for students, using prior knowledge and explicit learning intentions and success criteria to ensure they are setting and expecting high standards for all
- **opportunities for higher-order thinking and cognitive challenge** by designing learning activities and units long enough for learners to take in new ideas, link ideas, and use these ideas in a new way to do something with them in real life
- **opportunities for home and community support** and dialogue with caregivers
- **timely, useful feedback** that is explicit, proximate and hierarchical, allowing students to answer, "How am I going?" and "What's my next step?" (Alton-Lee 2003; Hattie 2012).

In addition, **direct instruction** and **learning to learn** using second language vocabularies are effective pedagogies for ELL.

Our experience is that all of the above are made easier when teachers and ELLs share a common language of learning like SOLO Taxonomy. This is because SOLO gives us a shared language that differentiates the cognitive complexity of any task and any outcome.

In the following sections, we share simple, practical SOLO-based strategies that enable L2 learners to build their expertise, confidence and engagement in thinking, speaking and writing using L2 academic vocabulary. These strategies include the use of SOLO academic verbs, process maps and self-assessment rubrics for teaching academic language and text patterns. They involve direct instruction and learning to learn strategies, which ELLs can use to learn and extend their academic vocabulary anywhere and any time. SOLO encourages ELLs to become lifelong learners in L2 and L1.

2. What SOLO can do for L2 acquisition and next steps

O le tama a le manu e fafaga i ia ma fuga o laau, ao le tama a le tagata e fafaga i upu ma tala.

Animals and birds feed their young with fish and blooms or berries of trees but the young of humans shall be fed with words. Samoan proverb (Le Tagaloa 1996, p 16)

Le Tagaloa's Samoan English translation, "the young of humans shall be fed with words", conveys the importance of feeding children with words. ELLs need to be further challenged, fed with words that develop deep levels of academic vocabulary, so they can experience academic success in the L2. Tracking progress and identifying next steps for learning are necessary for educators to determine progress (Murphy 2009).

In this section we look at how we might track the progress of L2 acquisition and determine next steps using SOLO Taxonomy.

Stages in language acquisition

The level of thinking and academic language required for any L2 task follows a similar progression in listening, speaking, reading and writing: from concrete recall through to more complex, abstract and conceptual levels. For example, when ELLs develop academic language in L2, the language moves from simple to complex in grammatical tenses, and forms vocabulary and meaning.

Krashen and Terrell (1983) describe the stages in the natural approach to language acquisition as follows:

Preproduction	Early production	Speech emergence	Intermediate fluency	Advanced fluency
Non-verbal response	One-word response	Phrases or short sentences	Longer and more complex sentences	Sounds like a native speaker

- An ELL may start with a non-verbal response – by simply pointing at, circling or drawing a picture to represent an L2 idea (**preproduction**).
- As understanding deepens, the student may offer a one-word response modelled on the teacher (**early production**).
- Thereafter, the ELL says phrases or short sentences prompted by sentence starters (**speech emergence**).
- In the next stage, the ELL uses longer and more complex sentences, expanding, elaborating on and relating ideas (**intermediate fluency**).
- Finally, mastering complexity, nuance and abstraction, the ELL sounds like a native speaker (**advanced fluency**).

As noted in Section 1, moving from early production to advanced fluency can take from five to seven years for children learning English as an L2, depending on their literacy levels in their home language (Thomas and Collier 1997). Low literacy levels in a home language and limited opportunities to learn at school undoubtedly make it difficult for some children to ever reach advanced fluency in L2. When we work with newly arrived Asian families, we actively address these issues by acknowledging, validating and encouraging children's L1. Some of the children undertook further learning in their L1 by attending sessions at the community-run Saturday School.

Although researchers and practitioners may label the stages differently, Table 2.1 shows that the gist of what they consider to happen at each stage is much the same.

Table 2.1: Different labels, similar stages in acquiring L2

Name of stage	Oral language output *The learner:*	Oral language input *The learner understands:*
Preproduction*	• does not speak	• little without scaffolds
Early production* Foundation Stage† Level 1‡	• says single words • echoes phrases that they hear • responds in their first language • participates using key words and familiar phrases • uses verbs in present tense	• individual words and some short chunks of language (formulaic chunks)
Speech emergence* Stage 1† Level 2‡	• uses mostly high-frequency words and omits structural words • uses non-standard vocabulary and sentence structures • uses the subject–verb–object structure if they have had a chance to plan what they are going to say • uses simple sentences • makes grammatical and pronunciation errors • misunderstands jokes • repeats or retells instructions using own words	• simple sentences and longer common phrases • short passages of natural speech, such as in conversations and instructions
Intermediate fluency* Stage 2† Level 3‡	• includes structural vocabulary to produce fairly coherent and accurate standard English • relies less on formulaic chunks and uses more independently generated language structures • makes few grammatical errors • can summarise instructions • can listen to the radio or talk on the phone	• some complex sentences • complete and incomplete sentences
Intermediate fluency* Stage 3† Level 4‡	• uses increasingly varied and complex language structures in standard English, with few inaccuracies • uses features of natural spoken language (eg, saying "coming" instead of "I am coming") • can apply the instructions and include details in more complex sentences	• connected text with several ideas or text sequences • longer passages of speech spoken at a natural pace and without planned pauses (eg, talks by visiting speakers)
Advanced fluency* Stage 4† Level 5‡	• uses increasingly varied and complex standard English language structures, with few inaccuracies • has near-native level of speech • can explain instructions using complex language similar to that of a native speaker	• complex, extended speech with a wide variety of structures at levels similar to a native speaker

Key: * Hill and Miller's adaptation of Krashen and Terrell's Stages of natural language acquisition (Krashen and Terrell 1983)
† New Zealand Ministry of Education English Language Learning Progressions (Ministry of Education 2008)
‡ Gottlieb's levels for assessing ELLs (Gottlieb 2006)

Stages in cognitive complexity of task and outcome

By thinking about stages of L2 acquisition in terms of SOLO stages, ELLs can think metacognitively about their learning (tasks and outcomes) and the learning process. With a SOLO-based language for learning to learn, they can ask and answer three powerful questions:

What am I doing? *(task)*   How well is it going? *(outcome)*   What should I do next? *(next steps)*

Our school uses the classroom-based approach to SOLO Taxonomy with ELLs. Students learn about the process of learning (declarative knowledge), how to learn (functioning knowledge), and when and why to use different strategies for learning (conditional knowledge). The model makes it easy for teachers to identify the cognitive complexity for different language functions (command verbs) and from there to plan appropriately challenging (explicit, proximal and hierarchical) "plus 1" tasks – or next steps for their ELLs (see Table 2.2 and Figure 2.1).

Table 2.2: SOLO declarative knowledge levels and ELL responses

Prestructural	Unistructural	Multistructural	Relational	Extended abstract
●	▮	▮▮▮	◆▮▮▮◆	◆▮▮▮◆⟲
Student does not respond.	Student response has one relevant idea.	Student response has several relevant ideas …	… **and** relates these ideas (*explain, compare* etc) …	… **and** extends these ideas by looking at them in a new way (*generalise, predict, evaluate* etc).
ELL does not respond.	ELL produces a one-word or two-word response.	ELL produces phrases or a simple sentence.	ELL produces longer and complex sentences.	ELL produces extended narrative.
Preproduction	**Early production**	**Speech emergence**	**Intermediate fluency**	**Advanced fluency**

Figure 2.1: Using SOLO symbols to indicate a learning task's level of complexity to ELLs

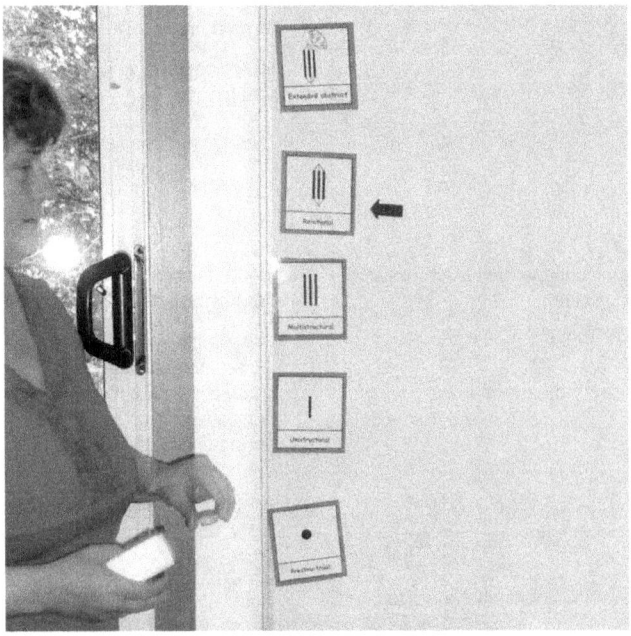

As described in Section 1, students and teachers can also use SOLO to look at the learning outcome's complexity. An advantage of this approach is that when the SOLO label sticks to the learning outcome rather than the student, the pedagogical conversation is all about how to strengthen or improve the ELL's learning outcome. For example:

>Teacher: What is the SOLO level of your work?
>Student: Multistructural.
>Teacher: Great – can you tell me why your work is at this level?
>Student: Because I have put more than one idea about my family on the Describe map.
>Teacher: I agree! Your work has several ideas about your family. Can you show me where your work is on the rubric?
>Student: *(Points to multistructural level on the SOLO Describe rubric.)*
>Teacher: *(Nods)* So what can you do to improve your work?
>Student: Use "because" to link ideas.
>Teacher: Great – let me know how you get on.

Co-constructing SOLO self-assessment rubrics with ELLs makes learning visible and helps them understand the role of effort and effective strategies in learning.

Learning tasks

Hattie (2012, p 54) describes SOLO as a powerful model for helping teachers to clarify learning intentions (learning tasks) and success criteria. Identifying clear intended learning outcomes – clarifying learning intentions (goals) – improves student achievement outcomes (Grant and Dweck 2003). When these tasks are further aligned with learning intentions and learning outcomes (constructive alignment), the L2 teacher can easily plan for deeper academic outcomes in L2.

With SOLO, ELLs and their teacher can look at the academic verb used and determine the cognitive complexity of the task. The teacher can then scaffold for deeper academic learning by using academic verbs to plan the learning experiences.

Table 2.3 shows how the verbs chosen for the learning task make the task's level of cognitive complexity visible to the teacher and ELLs across the scheme of work. Academic verbs are explicitly chosen to bring in ideas (multistructural), link ideas (relational) or extend ideas (extended abstract).

Table 2.3: Academic verbs aligned to SOLO levels

SOLO level	Symbol	Verbs	Purpose of the verbs	Phase
Extended abstract		Generalise, predict, evaluate, reflect, create	To extend students' linked ideas in new ways	Qualitative phase
Relational		Sequence, classify, explain, compare, contrast, analyse, relate, apply	To relate or link students' ideas	
Multistructural		Describe, list, outline	To bring in ideas	Quantitative phase
Unistructural		Define, identify, label, do simple procedure	To bring in one idea	
Prestructural		Misses the point		

When planning learning tasks (experiences), L2 teachers can use SOLO verbs to design "plus 1" learning experiences that extend the prior knowledge of their ELLs by one level (Table 2.4). Individual students may need learning experiences to bring in an idea (unistructural) or ideas (multistructural), or that prompt them to make connections or link ideas (relational) and to extend their linked ideas in new ways (extended abstract). In the process, all ELL students will be challenged to think deeply. The differentiated SOLO stations, in which students explore leisure time activities, illustrate this approach (see page 20).

Using the SOLO "plus 1" strategy (Hattie and Brown 2004) to select the appropriate level of challenge helps teachers scaffold learning experiences for L2 learners:
- Teaching without challenge risks boring students, who remain stuck with using conversational English.
- Teaching with an overly challenging level of academic language risks a lack of engagement among ELLs because they perceive the task as being "too hard".
- Teaching based on the SOLO "plus 1" strategy helps to find the balance between these two extremes, making it easier to identify more precisely the academic language that the student is ready to move on to.

The effectiveness of the SOLO "plus 1" strategy can be understood through Vygotsky's (1978) theories about the **zone of proximal development**; the zone where students can be helped to achieve deeper outcomes (Table 2.4).

Table 2.4: Zone of proximal development and L2 acquisition

Actual developmental level	Zone of proximal development	Future developmental level
Can do alone *Able to accomplish without help from others*	Can do if helped *Able to accomplish with the help of more knowledgeable others – teachers, more advanced peers etc*	Cannot do **Not** *able to accomplish even with help of more knowledgeable others*
Example: If the student can respond to tasks with one- or two-word answers ... (Early production – SOLO unistructural level response)	Example: ... then with help student can respond to tasks with simple sentences ... (speech emergence – SOLO multistructural level response). The teacher can prompt for this level of language acquisition by: • providing direct instruction in simple sentences and familiar phrases (formulaic expressions) • modelling correct grammar and pronunciation when using simple sentences to describe objects • asking questions that require description: "Tell me about Diwali. Tell me more ... Because ...?"	Example: ... but the student cannot respond to tasks with longer and more complex sentences, and cannot use causal explanation – how and why. (Intermediate fluency – SOLO relational level response)

Learning outcomes for ELLs

Using SOLO levels, a teacher can work out the oral and written learning outcome of any ELL learning task – declarative or functioning. Note that the SOLO level of understanding evident in an ELL's work always relates to the work or learning outcome – it is not a label for the ELL individual (see above). Two effective strategies for making the complexity of the learning outcome visible to ELLs are:
- SOLO self-assessment rubrics
- differentiating text by colour highlighting SOLO levels.

Sections 3 and 4 cover these strategies in more detail. Figure 2.2 shows how a task and outcome can be at different SOLO levels. SOLO self-assessment stickers encourage students to reflect on learning outcomes (Figure 2.3).

Figure 2.2: Declarative knowledge task and outcome can be at different SOLO levels

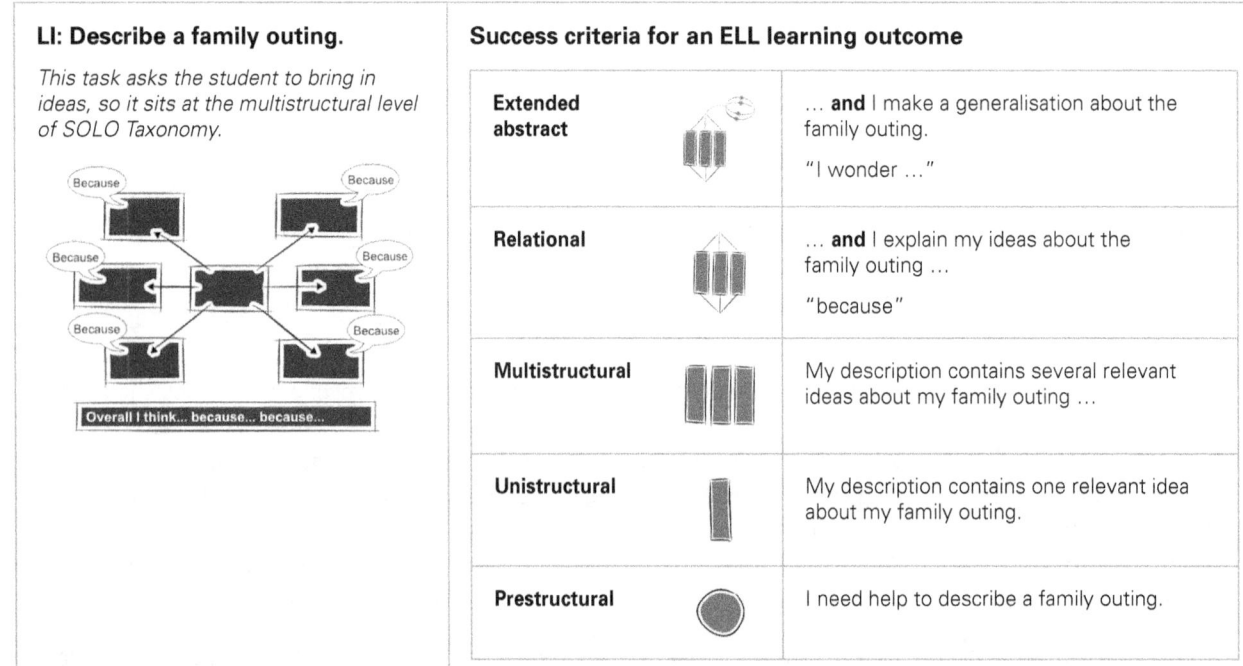

Figure 2.3: SOLO self-assessment stickers

| My learning outcome is at ▮▮▮ because _____ My next step is to _____ | ▮▮▮ **Multistructural** My learning outcome has several relevant ideas. My next step is to … |

Functioning knowledge outcomes for ELLs

SOLO functioning knowledge outcomes – levels of knowing "how to" – encourage discussion between teachers and students on the **effort** and **effective strategies** needed to progress the learners' ability to use the L2 when speaking (or writing).

For example, oral language development is a critical part of written language development. A fundamental rule for teachers in the L2 classroom is that **students must do *most* of the talking**. As well as providing multiple and varied opportunities for L2 output, teachers can use SOLO functioning knowledge rubrics to help students to think about their own oral language progress in L2. When teachers co-construct SOLO rubrics with children, in child speak, to make different levels of performance visible, they re-imagine the task through the eyes of the learners. From this basis, ELLs and their teacher can reflect on progress and better understand the effort and strategies needed to become skilled and active oral users of the academic L2.

A student's willingness to communicate in an L2 is based on many factors beyond simple measures of L2 proficiency, such as:
- the student's confidence and willingness to make mistakes
- the pedagogical approach used by the classroom teacher.

For example, if a teacher relies too heavily on an initiation–response–feedback pedagogical structure (IRF), where the teacher initiates, the learner responds, and the teacher gives feedback, teacher talk time can be privileged over student talk time, discouraging the student from participating. For this reason, pedagogical approaches that increase opportunities for student talk time are recommended – small group work, "think–pair–share" or "forced output" strategies. However, increasing opportunities for something to happen is not the same as making it happen.

Another way to encourage "willingness to communicate" is for L2 teachers to re-imagine "willingness" through the eyes of the learner. Co-constructed SOLO functioning knowledge rubrics differentiate learners' performance and open up discussion on effective strategies that encourage willingness at any level of language acquisition. Table 2.5 sets out an example of a SOLO functioning knowledge rubric for "willingness to communicate" with particular people in the class; similar rubrics can be created on related topics, such as willingness to share news in class.

Table 2.5: SOLO functioning knowledge rubric for willingness to communicate in English L2 with others

Functioning knowledge: Willingness to communicate in class	Prestructural	Unistructural	Multistructural	Relational	Extended abstract
Willingness to communicate in English with: • a teacher • another student or friend • a small group • the whole class	I do not like to talk in English with [xxx].	I can repeat/echo what is said in English with peer support before talking with [xxx].	I can talk in English with [xxx] but I worry about making mistakes.	I take every opportunity I can get to talk in English with [xxx]. I do not mind if I make mistakes because I learn from them …	… **and** I seek opportunities to engage in English language conversation outside the classroom. I actively encourage others to talk in English. I seek feedback on how I can improve.
Effective strategies					

It is possible to use SOLO functioning knowledge rubrics to look at L2 success:
- across each level of L2 acquisition (as in Table 2.6)
- when receiving and producing information
- when producing information (spoken and written)
- in showing social awareness of L2 culture when interacting with others.

Note: Although an ELL's willingness to communicate is important, it is unclear what form this active participation needs to take to promote L2 acquisition (Ellis and Shintani 2013, p 197). Most research has focused on the **quantity** of communication taking place – either number of turns or number of words spoken – rather than the **quality** of the ideas communicated (Ellis and Shintani 2013), leaving the practitioner to wonder about the preferred focus for active participation. However, if further research reveals that quality matters for L2 acquisition, then teachers can use the SOLO declarative knowledge rubrics described next to measure the quality of the communication.

Table 2.6: SOLO functioning knowledge rubric for different levels of L2 acquisition

Functioning knowledge	Prestructural	Unistructural	Multistructural	Relational	Extended abstract
Stages of second language acquisition	*I cannot do this.*	*I can do this if I copy someone else.*	*I can do this independently but I make mistakes.*	*I can do this and I can self-correct any mistakes.*	*I can extend what I do to the next level.*
Early production: one-word response	My response is non-verbal.	I can give a one-word response if I copy someone else.	I can usually give a one-word response but I sometimes make mistakes.	I can give a one-word response and self-correct any mistakes …	… **and** I can zoom out to using phrases or short sentences.
Effective strategies					
Speech emergence: phrases or short sentences	My response is limited to one word.	I can respond using phrases or short sentences if I copy someone else's formulaic expression.	I can usually respond using phrases or short sentences but I sometimes make mistakes.	I can respond using phrases or short sentences and self-correct any mistakes …	… **and** I can zoom out to longer and more complex sentences.
Effective strategies					
Intermediate fluency: longer and more complex sentences	My response is limited to phrases and short sentences.	I can respond using longer and more complex sentences if I copy someone else's sentences.	I can usually respond using longer and more complex sentences but I sometimes make mistakes.	I can respond using longer and more complex sentences and self-correct any mistakes …	… **and** I can zoom out to near-native use of language.
Effective strategies					

Declarative knowledge outcomes for ELLs

ELLs express declarative knowledge (knowing "about") in many different ways. The most usual ways are through oral, written and visual texts but gesture (pointing, shrugging) and movement are also used. We use the SOLO progression to assess five levels of declarative knowledge acquisition by ELLs. Table 2.7 offers an example of a SOLO declarative knowledge rubric linked to the acquisition stages of L2 language functions.

Many SOLO-based strategies can be used to make visible to ELLs the structure and the declarative knowledge process steps relating to the use of academic verbs and connectives. They include:
- colour highlighting SOLO levels and connectives
- SOLO prompts in sentence frames
- SOLO hexagons
- HOT and HookED SOLO visual mapping and self-assessment rubrics (see Hook and Mills 2011; Hook 2015).

Section 3 explores some of these strategies in more detail, before Section 4 examines the most powerful strategies: the HOT and HookED SOLO learning maps and rubrics for different academic language functions. The maps act as templates to record the draft thinking and writing processes needed for academic verbs (eg, *define, describe, sequence, classify, compare and contrast, analyse, generalise*). They are a simple, practical strategy to help make academic language accessible to ELLs.

Table 2.7: SOLO declarative knowledge rubric for ELL language functions in explaining causes

Prestructural	Unistructural	Multistructural	Relational	Extended abstract
ELL needs help to express an idea.	ELL's response expresses one idea.	ELL's response expresses several ideas.	ELL's response links ideas.	ELL's response extends linked ideas in new ways.
I can identify an event but struggle to identify any causes.	I can identify an event and suggest one relevant cause.	I can identify an event and suggest several relevant cause …	… **and** I can explain why these causes are relevant …	… **and** I can make a claim about the extent to which the causes impact on the event and provide reasons and evidence to back up the validity and reliability of the claim.

Strategies for planning the order and sequence of language acquisition experiences

Scaffolding L2 learning matters for ELLs. To raise achievement outcomes, we need the sequence in which we introduce learning experiences to support the learner's stage of language acquisition.

We have already identified the importance of:
- continuing to develop academic structures in L2
- allowing concepts and key terms to be discussed in depth in L1 (which sets up frameworks for clearer comprehension in L2)
- planning to maximise opportunities for rich oral language where students talk in their L2
- providing opportunities for higher-order thinking and cognitive challenge in both L1 and L2 (L1 is not simply a bridge for L2)
- encouraging home and community support
- providing timely, useful feedback.

Here we describe how to create a plan to integrate these ideas and maximise L2 learning using SOLO and constructive alignment. These plans can be shared with students and parents.

Constructive alignment

It is easier to order and sequence language acquisition experiences when teachers use SOLO Taxonomy levels and learning verbs to unpack the curriculum content or achievement objective. In using SOLO levels to further align achievement objectives and assessments, they use a process referred to as constructive alignment (Biggs and Tang 2007).

Constructive alignment is a principle that involves seeking the alignment of:
- what needs to be learnt (curriculum goals)
- what the students will do (learning intentions)
- the learning experiences provided
- how the learning outcomes from these experiences will be assessed or demonstrated.

After identifying an explicit learning goal (functioning or declarative knowledge) for students, teachers use SOLO and constructive alignment (Biggs 1999; Biggs and Tang 2007) to plan goal-focused learning experiences and assessment that will build appropriate surface, deep and/or conceptual understanding of the goal (Table 2.8).

Table 2.8: Using SOLO and constructive alignment to plan learning experiences and assessment – an example

Curriculum goals or achievement objective	**Learning intentions**
What do the students need to understand, develop or demonstrate? (Mastery goal)	What do we want the students to do to reach the goal? (Display along with SOLO level of task.)
Example Use academic language when describing.	*Example* Describe a sporting activity using academic language (bringing in ideas or multistructural task).
Success criteria	**Learning activities or experiences**
How will students know if they have achieved the goal? (Display SOLO-differentiated success criteria for task.)	What activities will help students in reaching the goal?
Example We know we are successful when: - *Unistructural*: We can echo what the teacher says. - *Multistructural*: We can make our own descriptions but we sometimes forget about the linking words. - *Relational*: We can make our own descriptions **and** use linking words like *because* and *so that* … - *Extended abstract*: … **and** we begin to use these linking words independently in our oral language and/or written descriptions.	*Example* Read and watch a video about a sporting activity. In a **think–pair–share**, describe what you have seen or read about that activity. Use a scaffold (eg, sentence frame with highlighted linking words or SOLO hexagons) to model a descriptive sentence based on the activity. Students repeat your example. Next students work in pairs to make their own descriptions. In turn, each student shares their description with their partner. Students share their original responses with the class, noting the highlighted linking words. Repeat and practise until students are using the linking words independently.

Note: For the HookED SOLO Learning Intention Generator, go to: http://pamhook.com/solo-apps/learning-intention-generator; for information on SOLO Taxonomy and writing learning intentions, go to: http://pamhook.com/wiki/HOT_SOLO_Presentations

The SOLO L2 lesson plan

The SOLO L2 lesson plan focuses on making meaning and form. It encourages planning for oral output and uses SOLO levels to prompt for higher-order thinking when making meaning at any level of language acquisition. It also includes prompts for the keywords/technical vocabulary and grammatical structures, keeping a focus on form, which leads to success for ELLs. Table 2.9 shows the plan contains the following parts:

- **What is the connection?** prompts teachers to use their knowledge of the ELL and the ELL's family to add authentic context to the lesson.
- **Learning intention (task)** and **Success criteria (outcome)** use SOLO levels to make the level of cognitive complexity in the task and in the outcome visible.
- **Function of language** encourages teachers to select visual mapping (HOT and HookED SOLO maps and rubrics) to clarify and support the purpose of the task and its various outcomes.
- **Prior knowledge** asks teachers to think about the level of L2 acquisition of their learners and their L1 literacy background so that they develop learning tasks that consolidate and extend students.
- **Structure of language** prompts teachers to create sentence starters, vocabulary resources and grammatical structures to support the academic learning of L2 students in their classes.
- **Learning experiences** prompts teachers to plan how they will introduce learning activities, balance opportunities for production (speaking and writing) and reception (listening and reading) and use assessment for learning.

Table 2.9: A guide to the SOLO L2 lesson plan

What is the connection?	Learning intention (task)	Success criteria (outcome)
How does this lesson help develop the big idea in the scheme of work or concept? *What is the connection to the students' lived experience/home and family?* *Learning is more effective when a link is made between a familiar topic or context and an unfamiliar one.*	*Create learning intention following the formula:* **[verb]** [content] [context] **SOLO level of task** *Highlight SOLO level of task.*	*Create differentiated success criteria for the outcome of the task at SOLO unistructural, multistructural, relational and extended abstract levels.* Unistructural or multistructural *Insert here.* Relational *Insert here.* Extended abstract *Insert here.*

Function of language

Select HOT and HookED SOLO maps and rubrics to support L2 learners with the function (purpose) of task identified above.

HOT and HookED SOLO maps and self-assessment rubrics

Bringing in ideas tasks	Connecting ideas tasks	Extending ideas tasks
	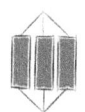	
Define Describe SOLO hexagons	Sequence Classify Compare and contrast Explain causes Explain effects Analyse SOLO hexagons	Generalise Predict Evaluate See–think–wonder Describe++ SOLO hexagons

Prior knowledge: Class profile: stage of L2 acquisition

Identify the L2 acquisition stage of students in your class and use the "plus 1" strategy to challenge them in their next steps.

- ☐ Preproduction (non-verbal response)
- ☐ Early production (one-word response)
- ☐ Speech emergence (phrases, short sentences)
- ☐ Intermediate fluency (longer and more complex sentences)
- ☐ Advanced fluency (near native)

Base this assessment on informed and accurate diagnostic assessment, not a hunch.

Structure of language

Select sentence starters, key words and grammar (including visual and oral prompts – eg, photos, videos) to support and extend the task for L2 learners at different levels of language acquisition.

Level of language acquisition	Sentence starters and sentence frames	Key words and technical vocabulary	Grammar in context
Non-verbal response – Preproduction	*sketch, circle, point to, show, choose*		
One-word response – Early production	*I saw a …* *My friend is …* *My name is …* *My favourite game is …*		
Phrases or short sentences – Speech emergence	*I saw a … in …* *The … was under the …* *… is similar to …* *… is important because if … was not there*		

continued …

Level of language acquisition	Sentence starters and sentence frames	Key words and technical vocabulary	Grammar in context
Longer and more complex sentences – Intermediate fluency	*The ... is a ... because it has ... and ...* *My problem is ... because ...* *In my opinion ... because ....* *Overall the big idea is ... because ...*		
Near native – Advanced fluency			
Learning experiences			
Introduction *Provide details of what will happen across the lesson.* *Include varied opportunities to engage with the same material.*	**Beginning** Watch the video of yourself dancing. Sequence pictures of the day.	**Middle** Add time order words, linking words and key ideas. Narrate and record each image retell. Write the ideas.	**End/plenary** Highlight the SOLO words, identify the SOLO level, explain why this writing is at this level and identify next steps.
☐ Receptive ☐ Productive ○ Experience-based activity ☐ Teacher-led ☐ Student-led	☐ Receptive ☐ Productive ○ Experience-based activity ☐ Teacher-led ☐ Student-led	☐ Receptive ☐ Productive ○ Experience-based activity ☐ Teacher-led ☐ Student-led	☐ Receptive ☐ Productive ○ Experience-based activity ☐ Teacher-led ☐ Student-led
AfL *How will you monitor student learning and decide on next steps?*	**AfL**	**AfL**	**AfL**

SOLO stations

In this approach the teacher sets up "stations" featuring differing L2 learning activities in the classroom or another location. Each SOLO station features a differentiated learning activity, so that it is suitable for ELLs at each SOLO level of understanding of the L2 task (prestructural, unistructural, multistructural, relational or extended abstract). With SOLO, differentiated outcomes are also possible so at each station the tasks can be achieved with different levels of success. In some cases teachers use virtual SOLO stations so that students do not have to move physically to the "station" of their choice.

To then run the SOLO stations:
- the teacher sets the number of students at each station, the type of activity and the conditions for moving to another station before the activity starts
- small groups of students rotate through the SOLO-differentiated stations and activities – throughout the lesson or across the week
- SOLO-differentiated success criteria are available at each station and self- and peer assessment is encouraged throughout.

With the differentiated learning activities, all students are challenged and can determine their own pace of learning.

Note: For more on SOLO stations, go to: http://pamhook.com/wiki/SOLO_Stations

The example of a SOLO stations activity in Figure 2.4 focuses on ELLs' leisure time activities. The station tasks are ranked to show increasing cognitive complexity. In the shift from unistructural in Station 1 to multistructural in Station 2, the complexity of the learning task increases quantitatively. In the shifts to relational in Station 3 and then on to extended abstract in Station 4, the complexity increases qualitatively. Figure 2.5 presents an example of a student's outcome from Station 4.

Figure 2.4: SOLO stations example – exploring leisure time activities

Station 1: Bringing in ideas tasks

1. Identify a game you enjoy playing at home. *[Unistructural task]*
   (What games do you play at home?)

Signal vocabulary: and, is, in addition, as well as, also, too, furthermore, apart from, in addition to, besides, what is more, not only … but also, another point is that, continuing on, for example, another, plus

Minecraft Football Chess Skipping

Differentiated activities

Preproduction	Early production	Early production
Point to a game or circle a game.	Say the name of the game.	Draw a game on a hexagon and write the name.
Preproduction	**Early production**	**Early production**
Echo someone saying the name of the game.	Record yourself saying the name of the game.	Complete a sentence frame: "I play _____"

Speech emergence	Speech emergence	Speech emergence	Intermediate fluency
Ask a friend to identify a game they like to play.	Record yourself saying a sentence about the game.	Take turns asking and answering a friend about a game.	Write a sentence about a game you play with your friends. Why do you think it is a game you enjoy? Use "because".

Station 2: Bringing in ideas tasks

2. Describe a video game. *[Multistructural task]*
   What is it like? What is the setting? Who are the characters? What happens in the game?

Signal vocabulary: adjectives, adverbs, above, across, along, looks like, near, onto, outside, as, below, beside, next to, over, such as, because, so that, between, usually, that is, generally

Academic language structures for describe
- HOT SOLO Describe map (*see Exhibit 4.1*)
- HOT SOLO Describe self-assessment rubric (*see Exhibit 4.2*)

Differentiated activities

Preproduction	Early production
Draw or look at a picture of your game. Suitable online graphics programs include: *[insert suggestions here]* Point to or circle some of the different parts of the game.	Use a sentence frame to draw or write one idea about your game. "My game is _____" or "My game has _____" Share your idea with a friend and the teacher. Record your sentence.
Early production	**Speech emergence**
Draw or look at a picture of your game. Name the parts and label your drawing.	Draw a picture of your game and add your recorded sentences to say what is happening in the picture.
Speech emergence	**Intermediate fluency**
Use sentence frames to write several ideas about your game. "My game has _____" "My game is _____" Share your idea with a friend and the teacher. Record your sentence/s.	Use the HOT SOLO Describe map to draw or write idea/s about the game. Use the "because" speech bubbles to deepen conversation. Use the ideas on your map to talk about your game, eg, "My game has _____" "I like it because _____"

continued ...

Intermediate fluency	Intermediate fluency
Use the cut-down HOT SOLO Describe++ map "See think wonder" routine to think about your story. *(See Exhibit 4.8.)*	Make a three-slide sequence or two-minute video describing what happens in your game. Use a HOT SOLO Sequence map and rubric to help you plan the steps. *(See Exhibits 4.3 and 4.4.)*

Station 3: Connecting ideas tasks

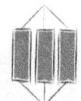

3. Explain why you and your friends enjoy playing video games. *[Relational task]*
   Why do you like playing video games?

Signal vocabulary: because, this is because, because of, reason, evidence

Preproduction	Speech emergence
How do you feel when you play the game? Point to the emoticon that shows how you feel when you play your game. 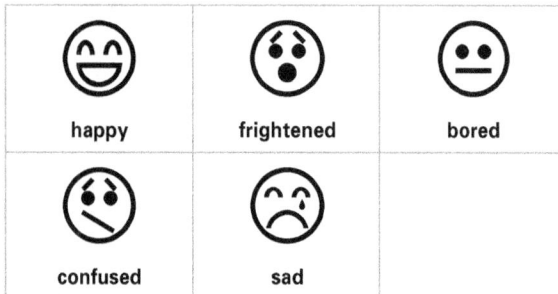 Mime the feeling and say the word.	Screen capture three events in your game. Insert these images on to SOLO hexagons Eg, Start screen, game play and final credits. Use the language of sequencing – *first, then, next, finally* – to describe what is happening at each stage. 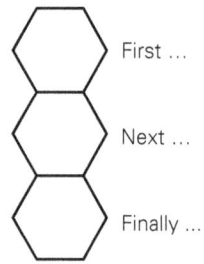
Preproduction Order three hexagons with images taken from the game. Echo the language of sequencing: *first, then, next, finally.* Eg, Start screen, game play and final credits. 	**Speech emergence** Mock interview. Work in pairs. One student interviews the other about their favourite game. Question: Why do you like this game? Response: I like the game because it makes me feel __ Question: Why does it make you feel like that? Response: The game makes me feel __ because ____ Change roles and repeat the interview.
Early production Use connectives to explain what the game makes you feel and why. "I feel __ when I play because ____" Share your ideas with a friend and the teacher. Record your sentence.	**Intermediate fluency** Advertisement. Work in pairs to make a radio or television advertisement persuading others to vote for your game. Use persuasive language: Make a claim and back it up with reasons and evidence: *[make claim]* because *[reason 1]* because *[evidence to support reason 1]*.

Station 4: Extending ideas tasks

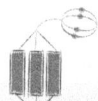

4. Create a book describing a game and explaining with reasons why you like playing a game.
   [Extended abstract task]
   Work with others or individually to write and illustrate an audio book about a game you like playing. Record your text so it can be played alongside each slide.
   Use a series of up to eight slides to:
   • describe and explain what happens in the game
   • describe and explain why you like playing the game.

Signal vocabulary: because, this is because, because of, so that, so, first, then, next, after, finally, overall I think

Note: See Figure 2.5 for an example of an outcome from this station.

Figure 2.5: Student outcome from SOLO stations – "Why I like Minecraft" by D, aged 6

1
Minecraft is a fun place.
By D

2
What is Minecraft?
Minecraft is a game that you can play on the iPad or on the phone.
Minecrafts has lots of things like bricks, bones, animals and water. You can build your own world.

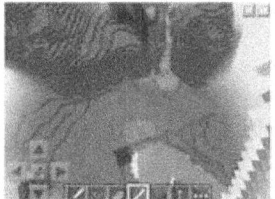

3
I can build a house in Minecraft.
I need bricks to build my house.
I have windows in my roof so that I can see the sky.
I have a door so that no one comes into my house.
I have put in some lights so that I can see at night.

4
I can make a bed in minecraft
I make a bed in my house so that I can sleep.
In the morning I can wake up early and I won't feel sleepy.

5
I can look after Wolf in Minecraft
I have a dog whose name is Wolf.
I feed Wolf every day because he is hungry.
Wolf likes to eat raw beef and he shares his heart with me because he is happy.
When Wolf calls to me that means he is hungry and sometimes he likes to go outside and run.

6
I can grow a tree in minecraft.
I can grow a tree in minecraft but I have to make it in one Minecraft day.
First I need some wood and some leaves.
Then I make the middle of the tree.
Next I put on some leaves.
I have to fly around the tree and put on the leaves because the tree is too high.

7
I can build a tree house in Minecraft
After that I build a tree house out of wood so that I can see far away.
Finally I build a ladder so that I can climb up to the tree house.
I have a chicken in my tree house so that I can get some eggs.
I can use my ladder to climb up into my tree house or I can fly up into my tree house.
I like my tree house because I can see far away.

8
Why I like Minecraft
Overall I think that minecraft is fun because I can control myself. I can control lots of things in minecraft like myself. I can build lots of things like a house, I can grow things such as a tree and I can look after animals like my dog.
I can press the buttons and I can control what I do.

3. Building academic L2

Or as one of my six-year-olds said on Friday when I was pushing EA thinking with my emergent learners: "Aww my brain hurts."

My response: "Yes this is brain hurting thinking and you can do this because you are ready."
(Sonya Van Schaijik, personal communication on extended abstract (EA) thinking, 2015)

General approaches and strategies

Even a most cursory reading of the research literature reveals there is no universally agreed approach to teaching L2. The field is notable for the number of different methods advocated and thus there are many different approaches for teachers to choose from. The approach a teacher adopts often reflects their own life experiences and their motivations for working with ELLs. For example, one author of this book explains her approach as follows:

> As a bilingual I believe the best approach is through additive language – bilingual education – where children grow up literate in two languages. It takes longer but the outcomes are much more successful. (Van Schaijik, personal communication, 2015)

On the other hand, some trends and principles have general agreement. For example, a greater pedagogical emphasis on communication and making meaning has replaced the earlier sole focus on grammar. It is accepted that the expression of ideas through "meaning making" activities can occur long before students have necessarily mastered the entire alphabet or writing system.

Our ELLs learn with others in technology-rich environments, with e-learning used in skilled and active ways to encourage collaboration and cooperation with students. Table 3.1 presents examples of applications currently in use with ELLs. Author Sonya Van Schaijik also brings considerable expertise and experience in building and leading e-learning communities not only within the school but also nationally and internationally (see her biography at the start of this book for more detail).

Table 3.1: Applications helpful to ELLs in e-learning

Fuze	**TimeBridge**	**Edmodo**	**Hapara**
www.fuze.com	www.timebridge.com	www.edmodo.com	http://hapara.com
Flexible video conferencing and online meetings. Students use it to share on the Flat Connections Global Student Summit.	Web-based software application for coordinating and running meetings and collaborating online.	The safest and easiest way for educators to connect and collaborate with students, parents and each other.	A highly flexible platform for teachers to create activities with learning pathways based on students' needs and interests
Google Apps – especially Google Drawings	**Popplet**	**VoiceThread**	**Padlet**
www.google.com/edu/products/productivity-tools	https://popplet.com	https://voicethread.com	https://padlet.com
Productivity tools for classroom collaboration. For example, students use Google Drawings to draw their own SOLO maps.	Mindmapping tool. Note: Students use class accounts under active teacher supervision because of their age.	Participate using voice, video or text. Note: Students use class accounts under active teacher supervision because of their age.	Online noticeboard

Get to know your learners

In our experience, the first and possibly most important predictor of successful L2 acquisition is that teachers **get to know the learners and build good relationships with their parents and families** (Table 3.2). As one L2 teacher said, "Do not think of it as welcoming a student to your classroom; think of it as welcoming a family."

Table 3.2: Key ways of knowing your ELLs

Learn to say hello in their language.	Know their home name.
Know their first language proficiency.	Find out their interests and build rapport.

ELLs' parents and families can play a significant role in supporting both ELLs and schools. Encouraging home–school partnerships brings learning advantages that go far beyond building fluency in L2.

One reason for getting to know your learners is that effective home–school partnerships **build the levels of literacy in the first language** that are so necessary for literacy to develop in the second. The partnership encourages ELLs to learn the L2 without detracting from their development of the first language (additive bilingualism). We learn to balance the culture and experiences of L1 with the new culture and experiences of L2.

Another reason comes from Patisepa Tuafuti's (2010) research into the "culture of silence" in bilingual education. Tuafuti found Pasifika parents often do not speak out when meeting with teachers about their children's learning. She describes "the culture of silence" as a Samoan perspective of "knowing when to speak and when not to speak" and "the social, political and educational factors in Aotearoa [New Zealand] that contribute to the 'silencing' of Pasifika peoples". When she created an "additive bilingual education programme, structured within a collaborative empowerment process of partnership with parents and communities", it unlocked the process that led to Pasifika parents' silence and their silencing and enabled rich learning discourse between families and educators.

Maximise use of L2 but keep using first languages

We encourage the continuing use of L1, balancing the ELLs' need for input and output in L2 with their need to continue to develop L1 (Figure 3.1). Where possible, we allow students to communicate key ideas in L1. Once the concepts are established, then they can transfer that knowledge into L2. If a child can read in their language, then we do not need to teach them to read. Instead, we teach them how to read English, which again means a transfer of knowledge.

We strongly believe that to reject a child's language in the school is to reject the child. We value all students' languages. For example, under the Ministry of Education's Asian Languages Learning in Schools contract, students have the opportunity to learn Mandarin alongside te reo Māori, allowing us to support Mandarin as the most common language spoken in our school and school community.

Figure 3.1a and b: Continue to value the use of the first language, particularly if ELLs are literate in L1

Use students' passions and experiences

When you know the ELLs in your class, you can **use content and contexts aligned to the ELLs' passions and experiences** to accelerate their L2 learning and to show and celebrate the gains they make (Figure 3.2). We have noted great advances in language acquisition when learning contexts are balanced so that they include students' passions, such as Minecraft, drawing, baking and video making. Shared events present further opportunities to learn (Table 3.3).

Figure 3.2a and b: Know your learner so that you can unleash their passions – ELL shares his learning with the principal

Table 3.3: Provide opportunities to learn from shared events – ELL writes on the Newmarket School Fiesta

The Newmarket School Fiesta
Learning intention: We are learning to use the elements of writing.
Success criteria: We know we are successful when we can: start a sentence with a capital letter; add a full stop at the end of the sentence; do not have capital letters in the middle of our words; use finger spacing between our words.
One Saturday the 16th of November at Newmarket School, we had a fiesta that started at 12.00pm
During the fiesta, the teachers helped at the fiesta because the art was from their classrooms.
In the library there was a bike and house products for the dishes being auctioned.
At the fiesta there were animals like pigs, chickens, alpacas a goat and horse. We could feed the animals and we could pat them.
At the fiesta we bought sweet lemondate, fruite kebabs and Korean sushi.
At the fiesta my class sold spinning tops and self-portraits.
Our Newmarket School children entertained the crowd with songs and music.
At the end I was tired because I had a busy time at the Newmarket School fiesta.

Share results and progress

Taking time to **share L2 learning results and progress** with ELLs helps engage and motivate learning as does **acknowledging and celebrating learning gains**. Balance opportunities for success with opportunities for struggle. With this shared information, it is easier to set realistic goals, keeping in mind the time and effort involved in learning academic English.

The following figures indicate how teachers can make learning visible by showing ELLs their results and the progress they are making against different measures, such as the Thomas and Collier (1997) chart (Figure 3.3) or the PM reading levels chart (Figure 3.4).

Figure 3.3: Make learning visible by plotting progress on the Thomas and Collier (1997) chart

Figure 3.4: Make learning visible by plotting progress on the PM reading levels chart

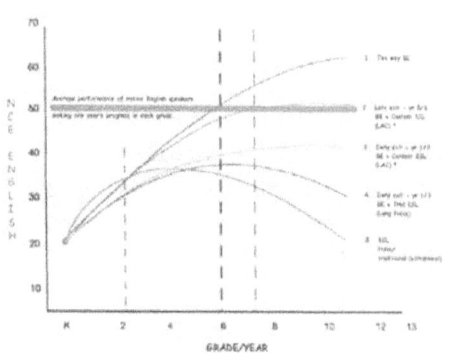

Balance receptive with productive activities

We match opportunities for L2 input (receptive activities) with opportunities for output of L2 production ("forced output") so that students develop grammatical competence. Achieving this balance is challenging in classroom environments, where talking space is often unevenly shared between students and between student and teacher. Given the importance of output, however, there is good reason to make the generalisation that, in a classroom with ELLs, students should speak more and listen less, and the teacher should talk less and listen more.

Some activities to help balance input and output are recording and playing back an ELL's message, Puppet Pals (an iTunes app) and VoiceThread for both production and reception (Figure 3.5).

Note: This is not the same as providing opportunities for interaction between listener and speaker. The output needs to be of good quality, rather than reinforcing mistakes and misunderstandings. When students interact with each other using strategies like think–pair–share, it is important to monitor the quality and quantity of language used (Ellis and Shintani 2013, p 219).

Figure 3.5: Balance learning experiences for production and reception – using VoiceThread

Note: For the complete presentation, go to: https://voicethread.com/share/7348267

Work on fluency but do not neglect complexity

To acquire academic use of L2, ELLs must master the complexity, accuracy and fluency of production. Fluency is the ability to generate a large number of ideas in a limited time. This need for rapid access to essential vocabulary must be balanced with the need to access complex and more abstract vocabulary and thought patterns.

Using leaderboards with individuals and groups encourages them to build fluency by competing against time or against their previous performance. Figure 3.6 shows ELLs writing as many words as they can in 20 minutes, while the leaderboard in Figure 3.7 presents the results of one student over time. In our experience, leaderboards offer ELLs additional feedback on, and reinforcement and recognition of their individual progress. Our students commonly experience leaderboards in gaming environments and are comfortable using them to challenge their own progress.

Figure 3.6: ELLs write to improve their fluency

Figure 3.7: Leaderboard tracks student fluency

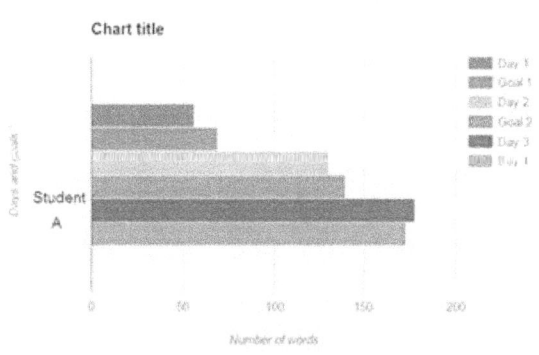

Celebrate effort when learning

Take time to notice the things that matter. Provide opportunities for all members of the school community to acknowledge students' success and effort. Balance extrinsic rewards from authority figures and stickers with intrinsic motivation by using SOLO levels to make individual success visible.

At our school, for example, ELLs and their families hold in high regard acknowledgement such as the principal's sticker and certificates awarded at school assemblies.

SOLO-based approaches and strategies

Among the SOLO-based approaches and strategies discussed below, some use SOLO Taxonomy to strengthen existing L2 strategies; others are new to the L2 classroom. With each description, we provide an e-learning tip.

Using SOLO in sentence frames

A sentence frame is a method of scaffolding to support academic language structures for speaking and writing. This framework or template supports and stimulates students' thinking while also exposing them to academic structures and technical vocabulary. SOLO-coded frames include explicit prompts for relational or extended abstract thinking that strengthen student learning outcomes. For example, we can scaffold writing by encouraging creative thinking with SOLO extended abstract prompts: "I wonder if …" or "In the future I think …" (see Figure 3.14 later in this section).

How and why is this strategy used? Sentence frames are used to support ELLs' oral and written language proficiency. The L2 teacher starts a sentence and leaves a blank line in the middle or at the end for students to finish. The following example (Figure 3.8) uses written language but visual language can also be used to scaffold student responses (see Figure 4.10 in the next section).

Sentence frames make visible to ELLs the explicit academic language structures for surface (unistructural and multistructural), deep (relational) and conceptual (extended abstract) outcomes.

> **e-learning tip:** Jo Davies' experiment "Telescopic Text" (www.telescopictext.com) provides a wonderful interactive example of how ELLs might elaborate on a simple text that starts off as "I made tea". Teachers can also use the site to create their own texts to model particular language features to their ELLs. You must register if you wish to save the texts.

Figure 3.8a and b: Using sentence frames (explicit text structure) and text highlighting

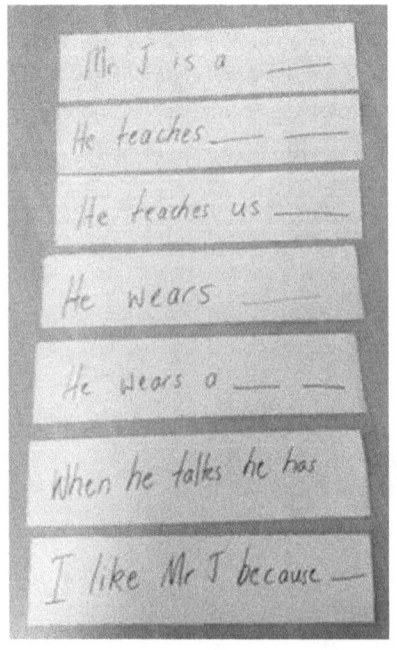

Using SOLO to highlight key vocabulary

Colour highlighting using SOLO is a simple strategy to make visible the cognitive complexity of declarative (written and oral) outcomes. Teachers and students choose one colour for loose vocabulary ideas (multistructural), another for vocabulary that connects ideas (relational) and a third to show vocabulary for extending ideas, subjective thinking and looking in new ways (extended abstract). SOLO highlighting helps balance the need for explicit instruction with free output.

How and why is this strategy used? Research supports the effectiveness of strategies like selective highlighting to help students attend to explicit text clues, such as when learning to make inferences (Reutzel and Hollingsworth 1988). In a meta-analysis of the research evidence for vocabulary instruction in vocabulary learning and academic reading, Stahl and Fairbank (1986, cited in Gu, 2013) claim direct instruction of high-utility words "has a significant effect on the comprehension of passages containing taught words". Furthermore, Gu (2013, p 308) claims that vocabulary learning strategies "ensure that students will be able to learn what to learn and how to learn it beyond the classroom".

In our experience, SOLO coloured highlighting helps ELLs to better understand the vocabulary and text patterns of academic language (reading, writing and oral language). Making visible different levels of thinking (surface, deep and conceptual) using visual highlighting of key vocabulary has helped build academic language in writing (Figures 3.9–11) and reading (Figure 3.12), while using sentence frames when recording oral language is a useful way of, in effect, highlighting key vocabulary in this mode (Figure 3.13).

> **e-learning tip:** In schools where ELLs are using digital devices (eg, a Chromebook), they can take advantage of digital tools that let them add highlights and text annotations to their own or others' work. They can:
> - highlight connectives that indicate they are linking ideas or extending ideas
> - add text annotations explaining the overall SOLO level of their learning outcome and next steps.
>
> We curate student voice recordings online in SoundCloud (https://soundcloud.com). With this audio platform, teachers can upload, record, promote and share their students' oral language learning outcomes. Teachers use an unpublic URL, given the ages of the children being recorded.
>
> Teachers are also starting to experiment with teacher accounts in YouTube (www.youtube.com).

Figure 3.9: Writing with SOLO highlighting – key vocabulary when describing an uga

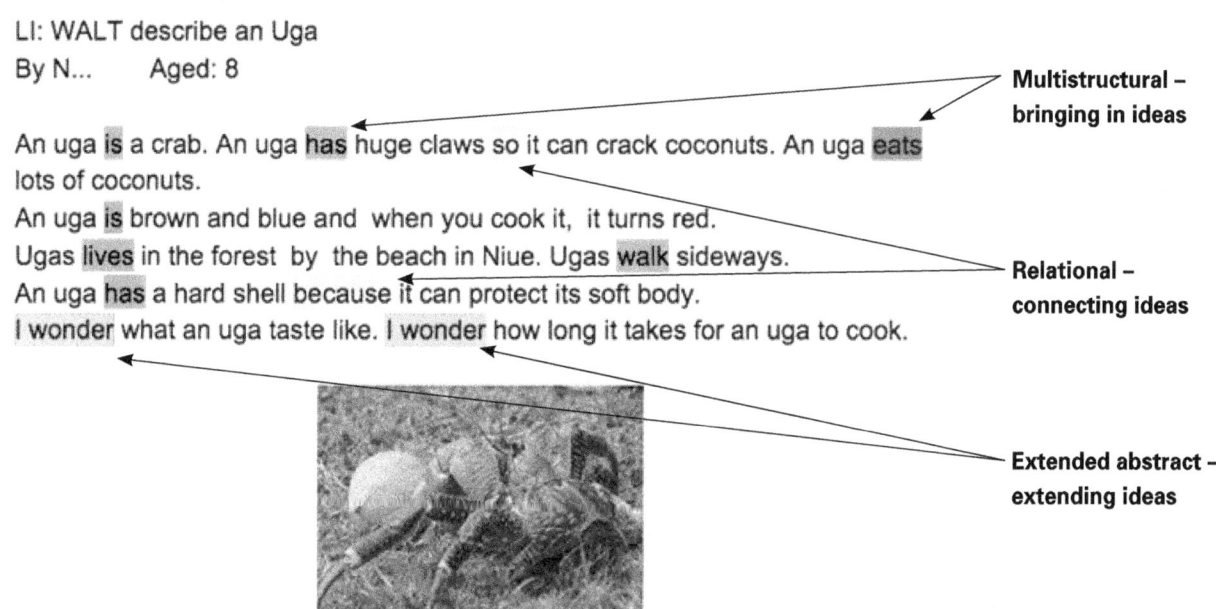

Note: Different colours have been used to highlight the different SOLO levels.

Figure 3.10: SOLO colour-coded display strips with key vocabulary to scaffold writing

Defining words	Describing words	Linking words	Time order words	Reflecting words
is	feels like	because	after	I believe
has	looks like	but	finally	I predict
eats	smells like	both	first	I think
lives	tastes like	different	next	In the future
can be found	sounds like	same	then	Overall
		so		I wonder if

Figure 3.11: ELLs using SOLO display strips as prompts for extended abstract responses

Figure 3.12: Reading with SOLO highlighting – students highlight key vocabulary

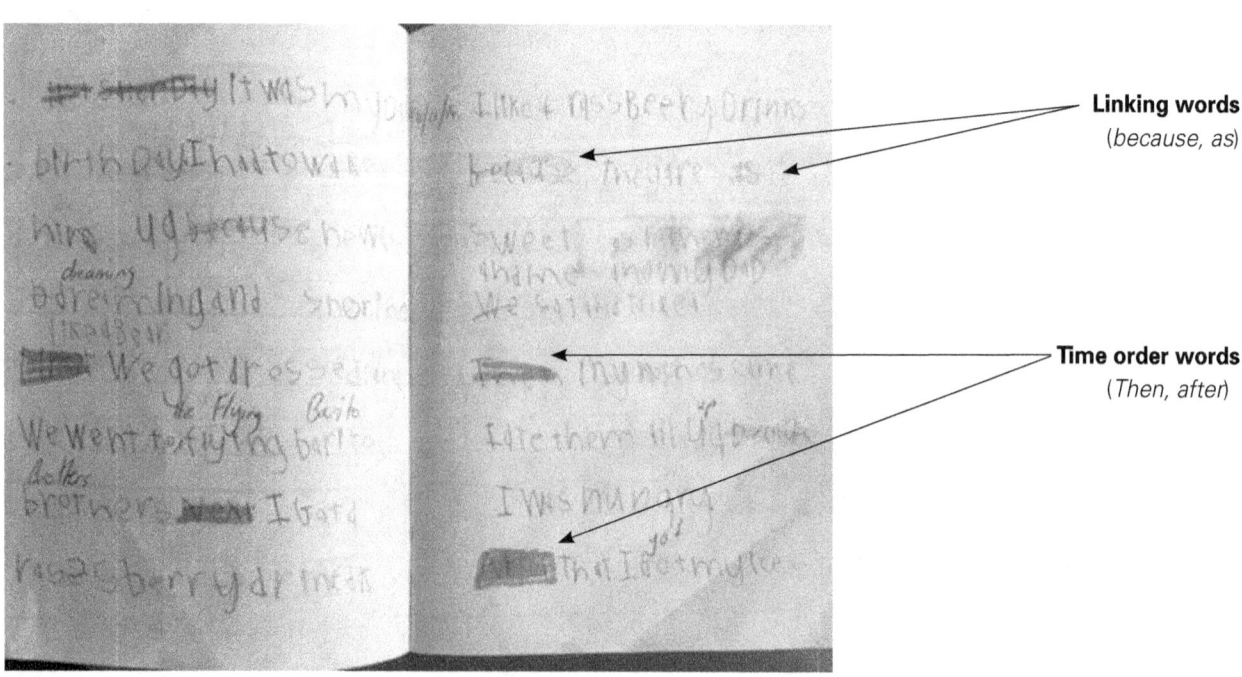

Linking words
(*because, as*)

Time order words
(*Then, after*)

Figure 3.13a and b: Using sentence frames when recording oral language to highlight key vocabulary – emergent ELL in Year 3 talks about a police officer's visit

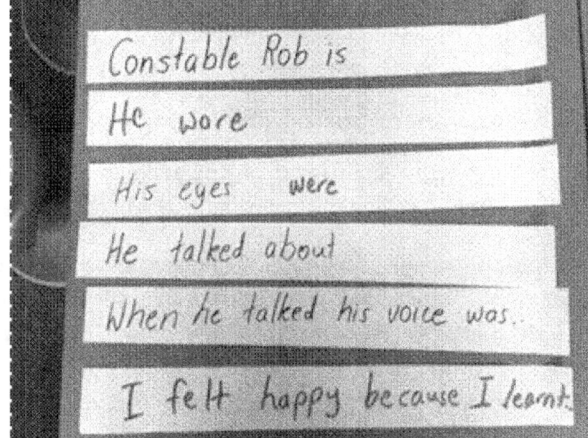

Using SOLO to reflect on learning

Another productive use of class time is to help students to talk about (reflect on) their learning using SOLO levels. As noted earlier, oral language development is a significant prerequisite for developing written language and this is enhanced when students can use SOLO levels to talk about the level of academic thinking shown in their learning outcome. It helps ELLs find their own balance in terms of thinking about next steps in learning.

How and why is this strategy used? Students use the connective vocabulary for SOLO levels to help them discuss the SOLO level of complexity of their learning outcome, either orally (Figure 3.14) or in writing (Table 3.4). This common language helps make visible to students the next steps and the effort needed to learn another language, which they may discuss in small groups and/or with their teacher. It allows students to see learning through the eyes of the teacher, and the teacher to look at learning through the eyes of their students. In time, students can then progress to discussing why they chose a particular HOT or HookED SOLO map to support their learning.

> **e-learning tip:** There are many ways to record student voice in the classroom. Author Van Schaijik prefers iRecorder Pro-Audio Recorder by SimpleTouchLLC (available through the App Store) because it is easy to access the sounds on the internet. Other options include QuickTime Player on a Mac, Sound Recorder on a PC or the AudioRecorder app on a Chromebook.
>
> You can also use Quick Response Codes (QR Codes) as hyperlinks to student audio recordings online.

Figure 3.14: Student talks about their learning from writing a description of a titoki tree – ELL aged 7 years

Titoki

LI: I am learning to describe the Titoki tree.

The Titoki tree is huge like a giant.
Its trunk is fat and it is taller than a house.
The Titoki tree grows in the forest and alone in the streets near Newmarket school.
The Titoki leaf is spiky and looks like stairs.
They are green and they can be as poisonous as uncooked pig's meat.
The Titoki flower looks like a star.
The colour of the titoki flower is purple and white and the stalks are green.
The Titoki seeds are black and red and they are poisonous seeds.
I wonder if the birds can eat the seeds because they look hard to eat.
We find the Titoki tree in the playground near the hall.

Note: To hear the student talking about their learning in this task, go to: https://soundcloud.com/nps_sonya/yuchen (QR Code also links to sound file).

Table 3.4: Using SOLO levels to write a reflection on the written description in Figure 3.14

> I thenck my writing abote, the Titoki tree is at extended Abstract because I used three or more describing words to discribe the titoki tree. I all so ust [also used] I wonder to thenck abot something diferent aboute the tetoki tree. My next step is to use time ordre words to put my ideas in order.

Using SOLO to vary opportunities to engage

L2 learning requires repetition (without being boring) to embed understanding and use of new vocabulary. Brown describes this approach as finding "old work new work" balance:

> Repeated opportunities for noticing language assists uptake, processing and output, consolidating new learning (Met, 1994). This can be problematic because some students require more repetitions than others (Chapelle & Hegelheimer, 2004) while teachers have limited time to cover the curriculum. Moving on is unproductive for English language learners who may have not mastered the previous vocabulary or syntax. Linking back to what has already been covered needs to be balanced against the demands for curriculum coverage. (Brown 2011, p 70)

How and why is this strategy used? It can be challenging to go over "known" material a number of times. Indeed, multiple opportunities to learn can become counterproductive if students go off the idea and become disengaged and/or bored. With different SOLO levels, modalities and multi-literacies, students experience "known material" in new ways. They encounter the same content through different tasks by working on a variety of L2 activities that support bringing in ideas, connecting ideas or extending ideas. For example, we balance old and new when:
- we use the same vocabulary in describing, comparing and wondering
- activities involve visual language, movie making, and using vocabulary in authentic settings like food preparation.

> **e-learning tip:** Record students' oral language and then use their video and/or oral recordings as a support and prompt to develop their confidence and willingness to communicate orally when bringing in ideas, relating ideas or extending ideas. This approach, using visual language and short video and creating narrative to accompany visuals and e-books, helps students use the same vocabulary or language structures in different ways.

In Figures 3.15 and 3.16, the teacher has recorded phrases individually and then put them together as a whole so that the student can "hear themselves" successfully saying paragraph-length passages.

Figures 3.17 and 3.18 show how video and digital photography, and food preparation are used to front-load technical vocabulary. Students identify the needed vocabulary in their first language so the strategy then becomes transferring vocabulary to L2. By taking lots of photos, you create further opportunities for students to engage with L2 vocabulary after the event.

In the age of the digital "selfie", some students are more comfortable with taking video recordings of their vocabulary practice or speech making (Figure 3.19). Hearing themselves also opens up an opportunity for self-assessment. As one student reported after hearing a playback of him retelling a story, "I don't understand what I am saying."

Figure 3.15: Using pre-recorded language to experience success – Maui and the Sun (YouTube)

Note: For the recording, go to: https://youtu.be/iuffMwq7Htg

Figure 3.16: Using pre-recorded language to experience success – Naughty Cat (Photo Story)

Note: For the recording, go to: https://youtu.be/PdRdcPCL99I

Figure 3.17: Using videos and visuals to front-load vocabulary   Figure 3.18: Using food preparation to front-load vocabulary

Figure 3.19: Using video to record a speech – student after one year at school

Note: For the recording, go to: www.youtube.com/watch?v=8P-D7G6Xeec

Using SOLO to set differentiated goals and success criteria

By using SOLO levels to set differentiated goals (learning intentions) and success criteria, it is possible to monitor and balance both **effort and achievement**. For example, a student's learning goal might be to answer subjective questions (extended abstract) using a "make a claim ... because ... because" sentence frame. They could then use:
- a SOLO functioning knowledge rubric to monitor their effort to reach this goal in class each day (Table 3.5)
- a SOLO declarative knowledge rubric to monitor how well they achieved this goal (Table 3.6).

Table 3.5: SOLO functioning knowledge rubric for trying to answer subjective questions using a sentence claim

Prestructural	Unistructural	Multistructural	Relational	Extended abstract
I did not make any effort.	I made an effort to answer subjective questions but only when prompted by the teacher.	I usually made an effort but allowed myself to be distracted by others.	I made an effort and used strategies to keep me focused on the task …	… **and** I encouraged others to find strategies to help them make an effort.

Table 3.6: SOLO declarative knowledge rubric for answering subjective questions using a sentence claim

Prestructural	Unistructural	Multistructural	Relational	Extended abstract
I cannot answer a subjective question using a sentence frame.	I can add one word to my answer. "Overall I think __"	I can add several words to elaborate on my answer … "Overall I think __ __"	… **and** I can add words to explain why … "Overall I think __ because __"	… **and** I can add words to justify my reasons. "Overall I think __ because __ because __"

How and why is this strategy used? It is only when ELLs and teachers monitor shifts in students' abilities to read, write, speak and listen that they can:
- determine if the ELLs are improving their language skills
- identify the strategies that seem to be doing the heavy lifting for each student.

It is important to provide assessment opportunities in reading, writing, speaking and listening (as in Table 3.7) because ELLs will develop their skills in each of these areas at different rates.

Learning an L2 is much like learning to play a musical instrument – it is hard work and time consuming. As the number of discarded ukuleles attests, the process can be disheartening, especially in an era that values the quick fix. When the teacher shares measures of effort alongside measures of attainment, students can better understand what helps them learn and both they and their teacher can create a balance between effort and attainment.

How can ELLs know they are making progress? The teacher shares with them baseline measures of their L2 proficiency – making learning visible. In talking with students about learning progress, the teacher also learns to look at learning through the eyes of the student and so is better able to determine any barriers to learning progress and/or more effective next steps.

Figure 3.20 shows two ways of tracking and displaying an ELL's progress in the number of words they can read (see also Exhibit 3.1 for a useable copy of the caterpillar learning log).

e-learning tip: Using technology like Hapara workspace (http://hapara.com) to curate many baseline examples of student work (involving both oral and written language), teachers can make comparisons that show explicit progress. One author shares early work with students after three years at school and notes the excitement of learners and their families at the phenomenal progress made. This is one particularly useful way to take advantage of the ease of digitally gathering and storing baseline writing or early reading. The children can then track their progress against their L1 learning progress.

Figure 3.20a and b: Tracking progress in reading with the caterpillar learning log and stickers

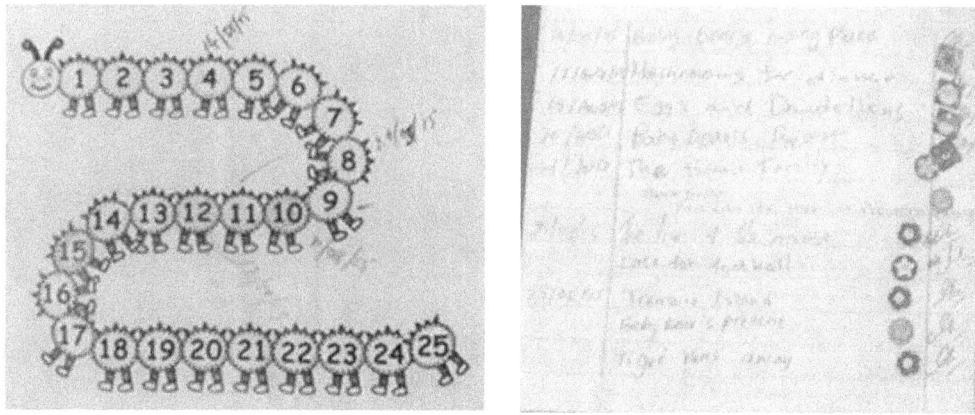

Exhibit 3.1: Caterpillar learning log for tracking progress in reading

Table 3.7: Using SOLO to differentiate goals in a listening activity with PM readers

Learning intention: We are learning to retell a story.

Session one
- Read the story to the children. As they listen, they number the pictures from the story in sequence.
- Read the story again and this time the children add the sequencing words.
- Together as a group, retell the story.
- Children use an iPad and iRecorder to record themselves retelling the story.
- As they listen to the recording of themselves, they identify the key vocabulary.

Session two
- Children use their numbered diagram as a plan for writing and they write the story.
- They highlight the time order words and the relational thinking words (shown as light grey and dark grey respectively in the following example of a student outcome).
- They include an overall statement that also has a big idea (circled) in the following example of a student outcome).

Session three
Edit, highlight and work the first draft. Listen to their buddy read their writing and make modifications.

Session four
Reflect on the piece of writing and identify the level using SOLO Taxonomy. Identify next steps.

Student outcome
One ELL has ordered the pictures from the story and annotated some of them with sequencing words: *First, Once upon a time, Next, Then, After, Finally*. She then produced the piece of writing shown below; her reflection on it follows.

The lion and the mouse

Learning intention: We are learning to retell a story.

By EY

In the green forest, a lion was sleeping on the soft grass.
The little mouse jumped on the lion while the lion slept.
The big lion woke up and caught the mouse.
At first the mouse begged, "Please don't kill me!" the mouse yelled to the big lion: He explained, "Maybe I can help you one day."
The lion began to laugh because he couldn't believe that a mouse as small as a rubber could help a big lion!
But then, the lion opened its paw and let the mouse go because the lion thought that was a such funny thing.
Next the lion laughed and laughed. The lion didn't notice that there was a huge net in front of him. So the lion accidentally went into the net.
"Help!", the lion roared. The lion realized it was too late and too difficult to escape. So the lion waited all day.
After that, the lion saw a small thing moving quickly to him…
The mouse came and it nibbled and nibbled.
Finally the mouse helped the big lion escape from the disgusting net.
The lion (felt) glad because he didn't eat the mouse. And the mouse (felt) glad too.
(Overall) a small creature really can help a big animal.

My Reflection

I think my writing is at relational thinking because I have used three or more linking words to link my ideas and three or more time order words to put my ideas in order.

My next step is to think more about my overall statement and explain more about the meaning of the story.

Using SOLO to determine prior knowledge

I have always been surprised by what students do know and by what they do not know.
(Brown 2011, p 68)

Prior knowledge is what a student knows and can do before teaching and learning activities begin. As an experienced TESOL teacher and academic, Brown claims above it is also about identifying what students do not know. Balancing what is known and unknown in both L1 and L2 matters.

How and why is this strategy used? Teachers use their information about what students already know and can do in their L1 and L2 to make pedagogically smart decisions about the appropriate level of cognitive complexity for the learning tasks that follow.

Knowing the level of cognitive complexity of an ELL's prior knowledge or performance, **especially in their first language**, helps teachers design individual and serial tasks that challenge the learner but remain within their grasp. For example, for a student whose description shows a multistructural learning outcome, the next step might be to:
- increase and consolidate the vocabulary available or
- suggest the student learns to link ideas through explanation using the connectives *because* and *so that*.

In our experience, when a teacher uses SOLO levels to determine the cognitive complexity of prior knowledge and shares this information with students, those students are encouraged to reach for the next step and the teacher gains support in designing the learning experiences that best help students achieve this.

Take time to find out what students know and can do in L1 and L2 before you start teaching. Moderate student work with other teachers. Consult with other teachers and family to gather as much evidence as possible.

e-learning tip: To generate SOLO hexagons for students to think about prior knowledge, you can use:
- Google Drawings (www.google.com/edu/products/productivity-tools) – in Google Drive, use the "New" button to create a Google Drawing
- the online HookED SOLO Hexagon Generator (http://pamhook.com/solo-apps/hexagon-generator), which exports content into a Word document, where it is possible to add images, photographs and colour, change fonts and so on.

How individual ELLs organise and tessellate the SOLO hexagons provides insight into the cognitive understanding they have **before** they start. You can then use this insight to design learning activities that both support and challenge students. Students themselves can use the tessellation as a writing template and come back to it to see how their learning has progressed over time.

Using SOLO when questioning

Effective use of questioning (number and type) is a strategy for building L2 proficiency. Balancing the types of questions asked is made easier with SOLO to categorise the nature of each question.

How and why is this strategy used? Hill and Miller (2013) suggest balancing the number and type of questions asked in ELL classrooms by using:
- first, explicit cues or **display questions** – that is, questions where the answer is already known (sometimes called convergent or closed questions)
- next, more open questions or **inferential questions** – that is, questions where students can identify the answer from hints and clues in the text
- finally, analytic or **referential questions** – that is, questions asking students to step back and analyse what is going on, create new structures and look at wider perspectives. Here the answer is not available from the text.

Display questions	Inferential questions	Referential questions

Table 3.8 links each of these types of questions to a particular SOLO level.

Table 3.8: Question types classified by SOLO level

SOLO multistructural questions	SOLO relational questions	SOLO extended abstract questions
Literal or display questions determine prior knowledge and check comprehension of the text. Their answers can be found directly in the text or experience.	**Inferential questions** are possible to answer using hints and clues related to the text or our own experiences.	**Referential or analytical questions** seek answers that lie beyond or outside the text or experience.

It can be challenging to design and ask inferential and analytic questions that prompt ELLs' higher-order thinking. Part of the problem is that educators have given a multitude of frameworks, categories and names to questions, questioning and questioners – for example, open and closed questions, fat and skinny questions, convergent and divergent questions, ignorance questions, fertile questions, higher-order questions, de Bono's Six Hats questions, Wiederhold's Q-trix matrix questions (Wiederhold and Kagan 2007) and Bloom's Taxonomy questions for remembering, understanding, analysing, synthesising, creating and evaluating. However, it seems likely that, regardless of the terms used, it is teachers' skilled and active use of questioning that is important in L2 acquisition.

Perspectives differ on what makes a powerful question. Ellis and Shintani (2013, p 214) report that some researchers describe the question in the IRF exchange as "a demand to display knowledge" and, as such, criticise its use as limiting ELLs in the range of language functions they can use and the opportunities they have for negotiating meaning:

> [I]n the IRF exchange, the student's response is hemmed in, squeezed between a demand to display knowledge and a judgement on its competence. (Van Lier 1996, cited in Ellis and Shintani 2013, p 214)

However, others consider the IRF exchange to be useful when the teacher changes the nature of their question or demand ("initiation" in IRF). For example, the question might raise an issue for negotiation or might anticipate a difficulty students will experience. Clearly what is important here is the nature of the question/s being asked in L2 teaching.

In our experience, SOLO can clarify some of this thinking about questions, their purpose and their use. With SOLO, teachers and students ask questions at three levels of cognitive complexity, as their questions progress from seeking surface understanding to deep understanding to conceptual understanding, as Table 3.9 summarises (see also Hook 2015, pp 30–31). These can be usefully framed for students as questions designed to bring in ideas, relate ideas and extend ideas.

A considerable advantage of the SOLO-differentiated questioning framework is that it can be used to plan questions to bring in, connect or extend ideas across all the different stages of second language acquisition. Table 3.10 offers an example of this approach.

Table 3.9: SOLO-differentiated questioning framework for three levels of cognitive complexity

	Higher-order thinking	
Surface understanding	**Deep understanding**	**Conceptual understanding**
SOLO multistructural level	SOLO relational level	SOLO extended abstract level
Questions to bring in ideas	*Questions to connect ideas*	*Questions to extend ideas*
What is it? *(define)* What is it like? *(describe)* What is it called? *(identify)* What do you know about? What can you see?	What caused it? What is a consequence? How is it similar or different? In what order does it happen? What is it similar to? What do you infer? Why do you think it is like this?	What is best? How effective is it? What is a new way? What is the overall picture? How did this make you feel? What does this make you wonder? What if …?

Table 3.10: Using the SOLO-differentiated questioning framework to plan questions across all stages of L2 acquisition

Stage of second language acquisition (after Hill and Miller 2013)	SOLO level of questions		
	Multistructural *Bringing in ideas*	**Relational** *Relating ideas*	**Extended abstract** *Extending ideas*
Preproduction *Non-verbal response*	Point to the picture that shows the cat. *(describe)*	Point to or draw a picture that shows why the cat was frightened. *(explain cause)*	Draw a picture showing how the story made you feel. *(reflect)*
Early production *One-word response*	Sentence starters: The cat was …	Sentence starters: The cat was frightened because …	Sentence starters: The story made me feel … because …
Speech emergence *Phrases or short sentences*	Using sentence starters as above: Within task, focus on description and using connectives.	Using sentence starters as above: Within task, focus on causal explanation and using connectives.	Using sentence starters as above: Within task, focus on expressing an opinion (generalising) and using connectives.
Intermediate fluency *Longer and more complex sentences*	What did the cat look like? *(describe)* Within task, focus on adjectives and conjunctions – *as, like*.	Why did the cat feel frightened? *(explain)* Within task, focus on adjectives and causal conjunctions.	How did the writer make you feel? *(generalise)* Within task, focus on adjectives and conjunctions.
Advanced fluency *Near native*	What did the cat look like? Give reasons for your answer. Make a generalisation about the cat's appearance.	Why was the cat frightened? Justify your reasons. Make a generalisation about the most important reason.	How did the writer make you feel? Give reasons and evidence to support your claim.

Teachers can use SOLO to keep track of the type of questions they (and their students) ask in the L2 classroom. One approach is to collate the questions asked during one or more lessons and code them against SOLO levels in Exhibit 3.2. By this means, teachers get feedback on the balance of the types of questions they ask when working with a particular cohort of ELLs so that they can continue to challenge students to think deeply in the L2 regardless of their level of language acquisition. Students can therefore practise thinking in ways that align with academic thinking.

The following examples demonstrate how teachers can use questions to prompt extended abstract thinking. Figure 3.21 shows a display based on "What if" questions about leadership while Figure 3.22 shows a student outcome from the "See think wonder" routine, which prompted for deep thinking in the L2.

Figure 3.21: "What if" questions about leadership to prompt deeper thinking for extended abstract outcomes

Questions include:

What if we wanted to be a leader and didn't first succeed?
What if we had a different leader each week?
What if a leader was caught doing the wrong thing?
What if we had to make new friends each week?
What if a leader doesn't listen?
What if we don't honour our promises?

Figure 3.22: Student's construction of extended abstract question, prompted by "See think wonder" routine

Sword exclaims: Spat *(Unistructural)*

Steve says: Kill the monsters because they will kill us! *(Relational)*

Wolf thinks: I wonder how I can got home. *(Extended abstract)*

Exhibit 3.2: Chart for monitoring the SOLO level of questions asked

Overarching question	Code SOLO level of each question		
	Unistructural or multistructural *Bringing in ideas*	**Relational** *Linking ideas*	**Extended abstract** *Extending ideas*
Example How can we keep the air we breathe clean and healthy?	What is unclean or unhealthy air like? (Describe unclean or unhealthy air.)	What makes our air unclean or unhealthy? (Explain reasons for unclean or unhealthy air.)	How can we improve the quality of the air we breathe (make it cleaner and healthier)? (Make a generalisation about improving air quality.)
Total questions asked			
Teacher reflection: How well do the types of questions asked meet the learning needs of my ELLs?			

When ELLs develop enough fluency in L2, they can monitor their own questioning behaviours. For example, the following students used the HookED SOLO Question App (see e-learning tip below) to help them frame their questions when interviewing an air scientist via Skype. Their questions included the following:

Student A: Can you explain what PM2.5 is and what causes it in Auckland's air? (Multistructural/relational)

Student B: What city has a similar air quality to Auckland? (Relational)

Student C: What do you predict Auckland's air quality will be like in 10 years' time? (Extended abstract)

Student A::How could we reverse the effects of Auckland's air quality? (Extended abstract)

Student B: What is your opinion about Auckland air quality? (Extended abstract)

Student C: How long before we get to see Auckland's air quality in real time like we can in other cities? (Multistructural)

e-learning tip: Through Skype, connect with a high-interest audience, such as another class, for students to try out their questioning skills (Figure 3.23). Student-generated questions for another class tend to be at a multistructural level.

Teachers and students can use the HookED SOLO Question App for iPad (available at the App Store) to learn how to ask the questions that matter most at different SOLO levels. Use the SOLO-coded question banks within the app or create your own; either way you will develop relevant, appropriate and substantial questions.

Figure 3.23: ELLs Skyping with another class to ask questions for Julie Lindsay's Flat Connections Project

Using SOLO hexagons

SOLO hexagons (based on an idea from Hodgson 1992) provide a strategy for enhancing higher-order thinking and systems thinking in individual work and small-group discussion. They are a pedagogical approach offering balance in many guises:
- Teachers in general use them to determine prior knowledge, scaffold student writing and oral language, conduct formative assessment, and revise and/or extend student thinking.
- L2 teachers in particular use them to develop fluency in formulaic expressions and rule-based competence.

How and why is this strategy used? In our experience, SOLO hexagons are a powerful support for ELLs, offering them diverse opportunities to practise oral language and higher-order thinking. The general process for using them is as follows:
1. Teachers and/or students generate content (symbols, ideas, text and images) on hexagons.
2. Students identify and describe the content on each hexagon.
3. Students make links between the hexagons, annotating any links with reasons.
4. Students extend their thinking by making a generalisation about the big idea in any cluster or clusters of hexagons.

Challenging other ELLs to look for connections and extend their thinking is easy and fun! Students share their loose hexagons, and challenge others to make connections and extend the ideas (Figure 3.24).

The outcomes from this activity (Figure 3.25) can be added to over time as vocabulary and understanding grow. The addition of new content shows progress in students' L2 acquisition. The final tessellations are great to then use as a prompt for oral language and early writing.

Figure 3.24a and b: SOLO hexagons prompt ELLs to use oral language when negotiating the reasons for connecting ideas

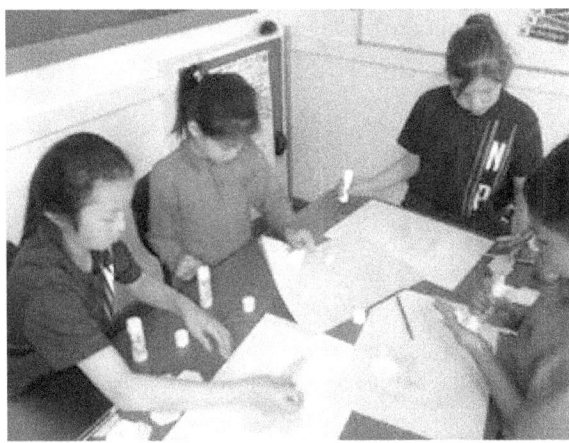

Figure 3.25: Display of student work using SOLO hexagons and SOLO vocabulary strips to describe a moment in time

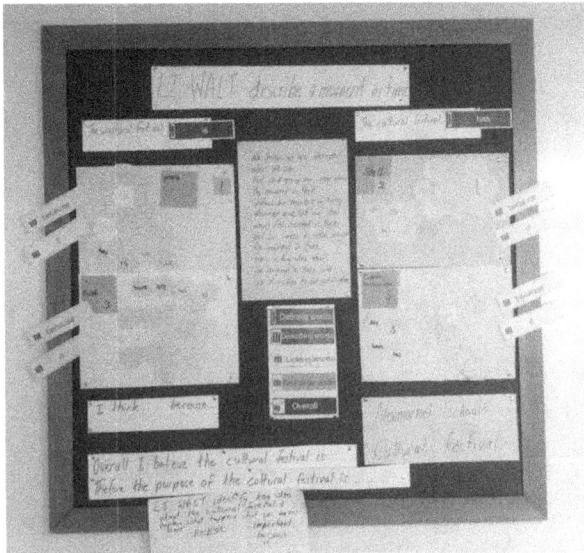

Using a simple HookED SOLO rubric (Exhibit 3.3), students can reflect on whether their outcome from the activity is:
- **prestructural** – they have no relevant ideas on the hexagons
- **unistructural** – they have one relevant idea on a hexagon – surface thinking
- **multistructural** – they have many relevant ideas on the hexagons – surface thinking
- **relational** – they have linked or related ideas on the hexagons – deep thinking
- **extended abstract** – they have extended ideas about the clusters of hexagons – big picture conceptual thinking.

> **e-learning tip:** Use any of the following online hexagon resources:
> - HookED SOLO Hexagon Generator http://pamhook.com/solo-apps/hexagon-generator
> - SOLO Hexagon template for primary schools:
>   http://pamhook.com/wiki/File:HookED_SOLO_Hexagons_Template_Primary_Y012.pdf
> - SOLO Hexagon template for secondary schools:
>   http://pamhook.com/wiki/File:HookED_SOLO_Hexagons_Template_Secondary.pdf

Exhibit 3.3: HookED SOLO hexagons rubric

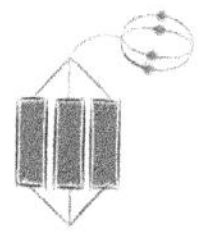	... **and** I can make a generalisation about the linked ideas.	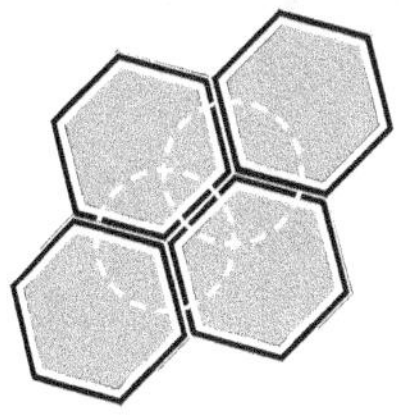
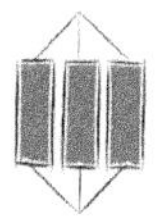	... **and** I can make connections between the ideas and explain why ...	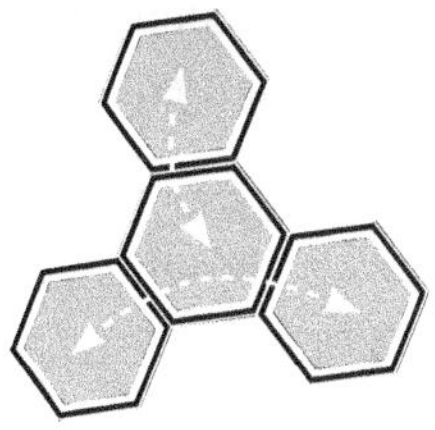
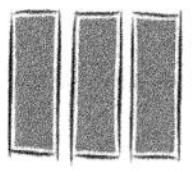	I have several relevant ideas ...	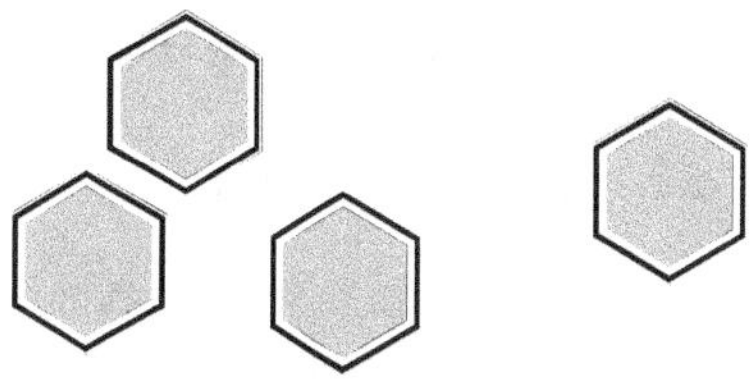
	I have one relevant idea.	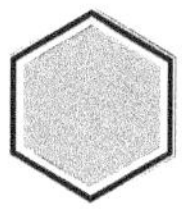
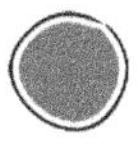	I need help to start.	

My learning outcome is _____ because _____

My next step is to _____

© HookED, Pam Hook 2016. All rights reserved.

4. Text patterns for academic English

O le tele o sulu, e maua ai figota.
The more torches there are, the greater the light, which brings a more abundant catch.
(Ministry of Education 2009, pp 10, 103)

HOT and HookED SOLO process maps and self-assessment rubrics (Hook and Mills 2011; Hook 2015) offer strategies (torches) to help students develop deep understanding of text patterns for academic language function and structure. SOLO process maps act as visual templates for draft thinking and writing using academic (or command) verbs.

In our experience, the SOLO maps and rubrics make it easier for teachers and ELLs to identify the academic language functions (the purpose for which we are using the language), and the academic language structure of tasks, at different stages of L2 acquisition.

This section presents common text patterns for:
- bringing in ideas (multistructural)
- linking ideas (relational)
- extending ideas (extended abstract).

It links these text patterns to a range of SOLO strategies. A particular focus is SOLO maps and rubrics that provide explicit visual summaries (maps) and differentiated success criteria (self-assessment rubrics).

Note: For a wide range of SOLO maps and rubrics that can be photocopied, see Hook and Mills (2011) and Hook (2015).

Text patterns for bringing in ideas (multistructural tasks)

Language function: Bringing in ideas (unistructural or multistructural task) – surface thinking
Language functions that help ELLs bring in ideas include tasks using academic verbs such as *define, describe, identify, name, list, label, elaborate*.

Language structure: Loose ideas
Language structures that help ELLs bring in ideas include sentence starters and sentence frames, key words and appropriate grammar (as in Table 4.1).

This subsection focuses on the task of *describing* to illustrate how SOLO strategies such as SOLO maps, as visual summaries of text patterns for bringing in ideas, can support this task.

Describing with SOLO strategies

Description is a powerful text pattern for ELLs who wish to acquire academic English. When they can describe in skilled and active ways, students gather information about the relevant attributes of a word or term and use these in any logical order to describe an object, place, event and so on. A HOT SOLO Describe map (Exhibit 4.1) and sentence frames (Table 4.1) support them in their describing task.

Exhibit 4.2 presents a HOT SOLO Describe self-assessment rubric, which the teacher and ELL can use to identify the SOLO level of the ELL's description. You can see an example of how to apply this approach in Table 4.2, which gives examples of ELL descriptions, along with effective prompts, at each SOLO level.

A range of examples of ELLs' descriptive work then follows.

Exhibit 4.1: HOT SOLO Describe map as a multistructural supporting strategy

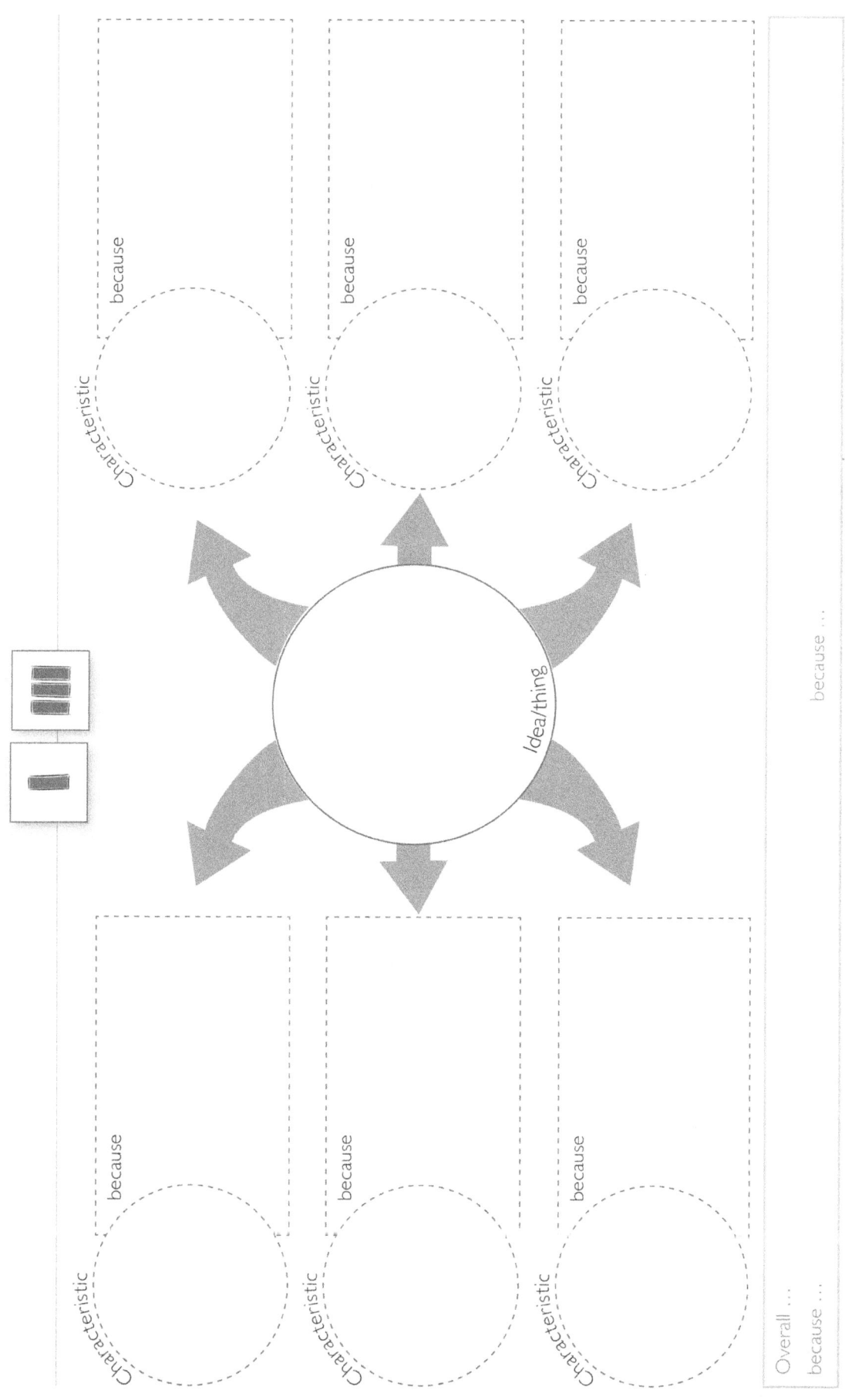

© Hooked-on-Thinking. Pam Hook and Julie Mills, 2011. All rights reserved.

Table 4.1: Supporting language structures for a describing task

Function: Describe		Question: What is it like?
Sentence starters and sentence frames	Key words	Grammar
It looks like ... It contains ... It shows ... In addition, it has ... It has ... and ... It consists of ... It is known for ... It is characterised by being ... and ... It is identified by ... For instance, it has ... and ... For example, it shows ... and ...	above, across, along, appears to be, as in, behind, before, beside, between, down, at the back of, in front of, looks like, near, on top of, onto, outside, over, such as, to the right, to the left, under	Word order

Exhibit 4.2: HOT SOLO Describe self-assessment rubric for SOLO-differentiated outcomes

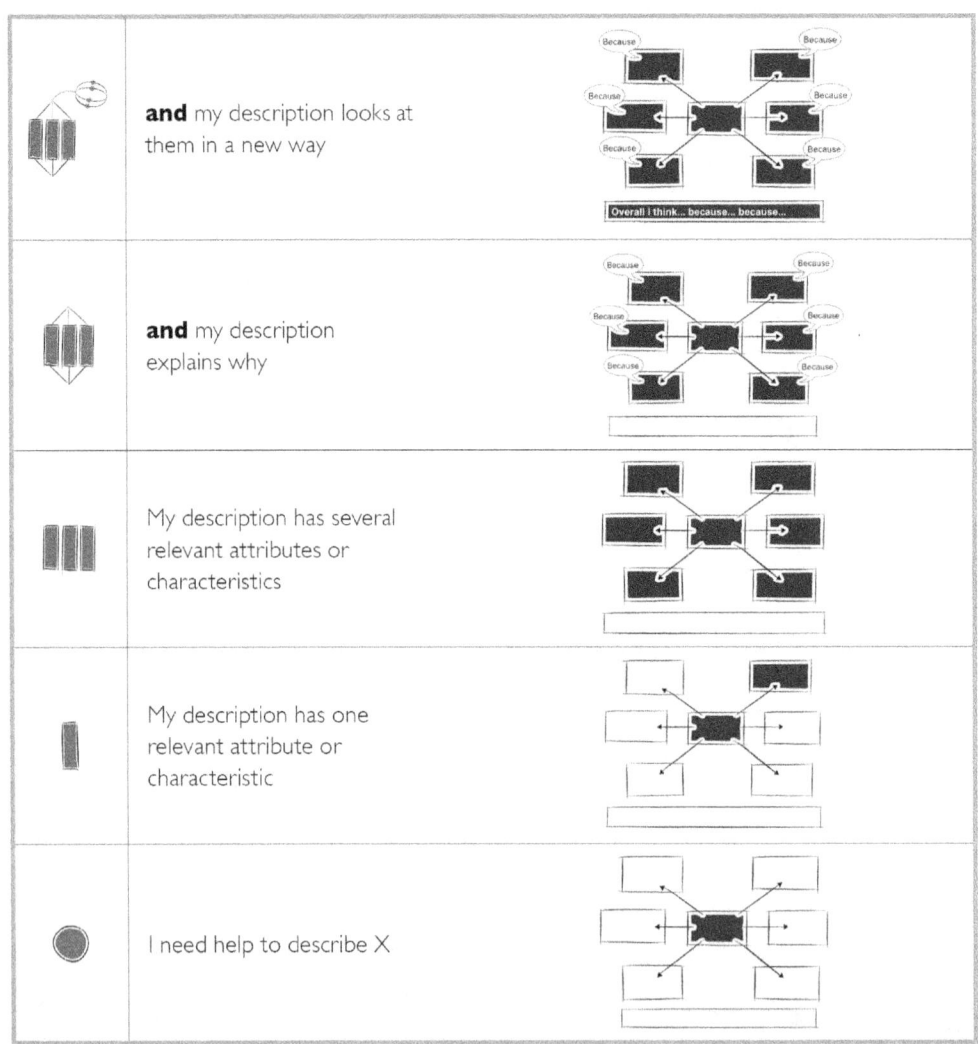

SOLO learning log

My description is at a _____ SOLO level outcome because ...

My next step is to ...

© Hooked-on-Thinking. Pam Hook and Julie Mills, 2011. All rights reserved.

Table 4.2: Applying the HOT SOLO Describe self-assessment rubric to ELL descriptions

SOLO level	Learning outcome	Effective prompts	Example of ELL work at this level
Prestructural	The student points or draws. **(Preproduction)**	Show me … Draw …	
Unistructural	The student describes the object, event, place or person using an adjective or adjectival phrase. **(Early production)**	Is it fun or boring? What is that?	fun building blocks
Multistructural	The student describes the object, event, place or person using several adjectives in phrases or short sentences … **(Speech emergence)**	What is it like? What do you do?	The computer game is fun. I use the building blocks.
Relational	… **and** the student elaborates on the description using longer sentences and offering an explanation (using *because/ so that*) … **(Intermediate fluency)**	Why do you like it?	The computer game is fun *because* you can use the building blocks to make things.
Extended abstract	… **and** the student can make claims about the description of the object, event, place or person (double *because* structure). **(Advanced fluency)**	Why do you think it makes you happy?	[Same as relational plus …] Playing the game makes me happy *because* I make things with my friends *because* you can switch to two-player mode.

Example: Modelling how to write a description

This example shows how teachers can model writing a description following these steps:
1. Co-construct a HOT SOLO Describe map (Figure 4.1).
2. Put the ideas in order and identify the key idea (Figure 4.2).
3. Students independently write a description, using SOLO highlighting to identify relational and extended abstract thinking (Figure 4.3).

Figure 4.1: Co-construct a SOLO Describe map for describing a monarch butterfly

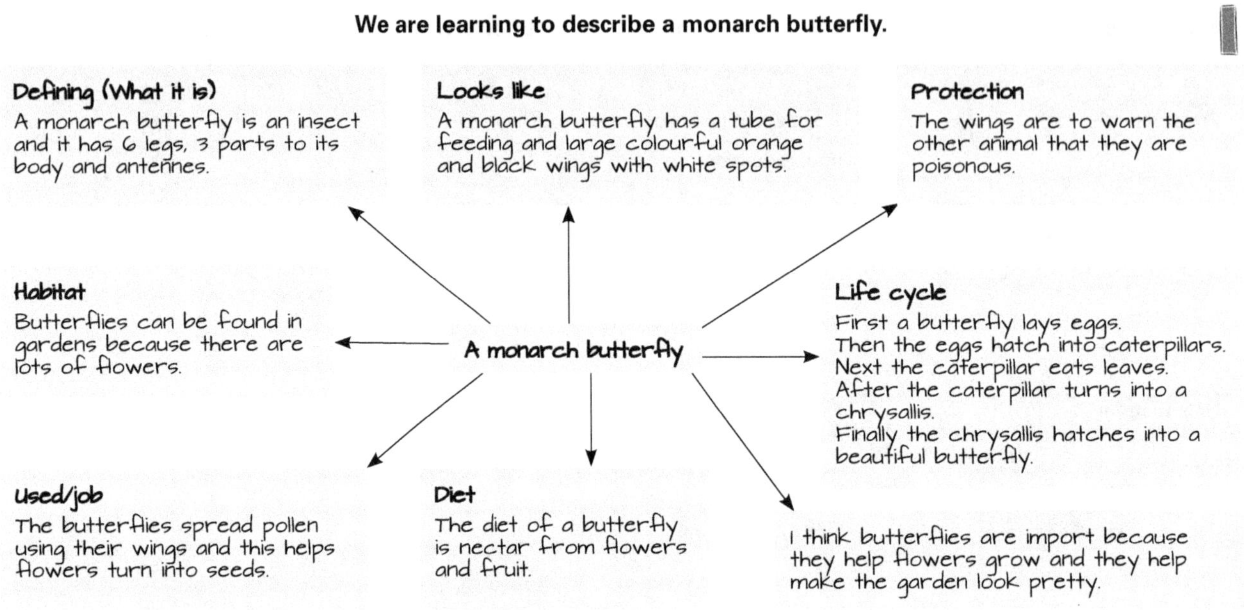

We are learning to describe a monarch butterfly.
Defining (What it is)
A monarch butterfly is an insect and it has 6 legs, 3 parts to its body and antennes.
Looks like
A monarch butterfly has a tube for feeding and large colourful orange and black wings with white spots.
Protection
The wings are to warn the other animal that they are poisonous.
Habitat
Butterflies can be found in gardens because there are lots of flowers.
A monarch butterfly
Life cycle
First a butterfly lays eggs.
Then the eggs hatch into caterpillars.
Next the caterpillar eats leaves.
After the caterpillar turns into a chrysallis.
Finally the chrysallis hatches into a beautiful butterfly.
Used/job
The butterflies spread pollen using their wings and this helps flowers turn into seeds.
Diet
The diet of a butterfly is nectar from flowers and fruit.
I think butterflies are import because they help flowers grow and they help make the garden look pretty.

Figure 4.2: Student sorts the cut-out paragraphs and then adds key vocabulary

A monarch butterfly is an insect. It has six legs and three parts to its body and antennas
A monarch has a tube for feeding and has large colourful orange and black wings with white spots.
Butterflies can be found in gardens because there are lots of flowers.
A butterfly eats necter from flowers and fruit. It does this by sucking the juice through its mouth straw.
First a butterfly lays eggs. Then the eggs hatch into caterpillars. Next the caterpillar eats leaves. After that the caterpillar turns into a chrysalis. Finally the chrysalis hatches into a beautiful butterfly.
The butterfly spreads pollen using their wings and this helps flowers turn into seeds.

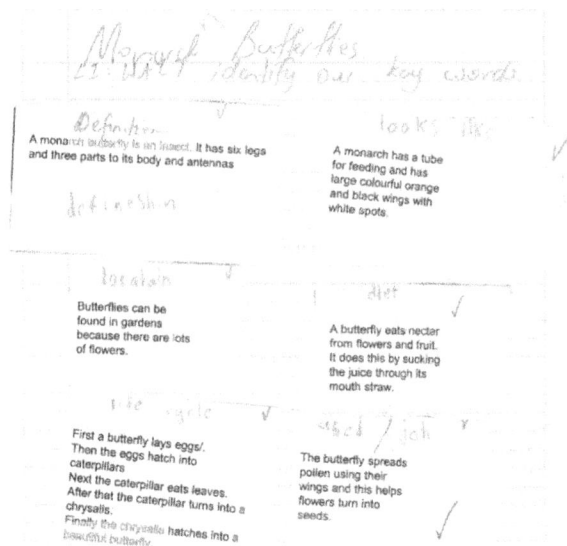

Figure 4.3: Student's independent description of a monarch butterfly, with SOLO highlighting

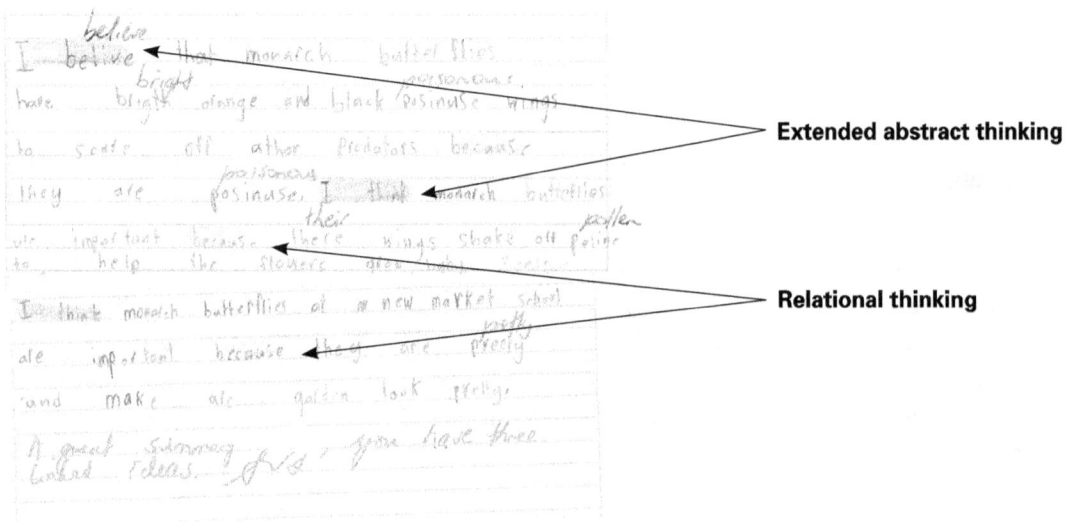

Extended abstract thinking
Relational thinking

Other examples of ELL descriptions using SOLO strategies

The following examples demonstrate:

- a student's description of a lemon, based on a plan made using a SOLO Describe map (Figure 4.4)
- a student's description of the Governor General, which was personally signed by him as part of making the study of leaders real for ELLs by inviting leaders to visit and view students' work (Figure 4.5)
- a nine-year-old student's construction of a SOLO hexagon grid, made with Google Drawings, which is used effectively as a SOLO Describe map to plan a description (Figure 4.6)
- the resulting description of a cultural festival, based on the SOLO hexagon plan (Figure 4.7). A peer assessment is also included, identifying the SOLO level of the description and giving reasons for that choice.

Figure 4.4: Description of a lemon, planned with SOLO Describe map

Name: S........
Learning intention: We are learning to describe a lemon.
A lemon is a type of yellow and oval fruit.
A lemon is juicy and sour. At the end of the lemon it has a pointy bit like a pointed cone.
A lemon is heavy like a heavy small rock.
The lemon juice is sticky like melted chocolate.
Inside the lemon it has some seeds.
When you cut the lemon, it looks like a circle.
When I squeezed the lemon some juice came spitting out.
We went to the staff room and added honey and boiling water to the lemon juice to make it taste better.

Figure 4.5: Description of the Governor General, planned with SOLO Describe map

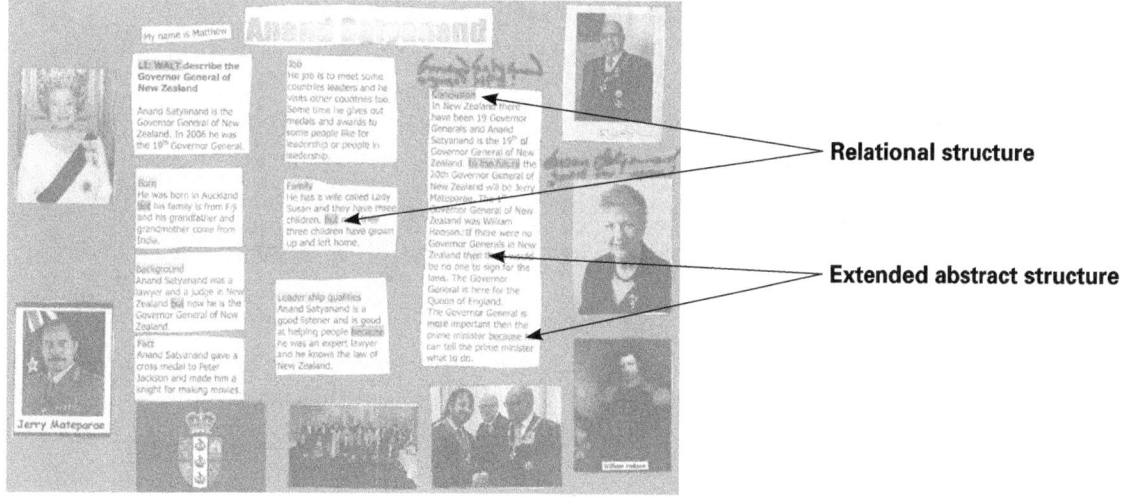

Figure 4.6: Using SOLO hexagons with colour coding as a SOLO Describe map to plan a description of a cultural festival

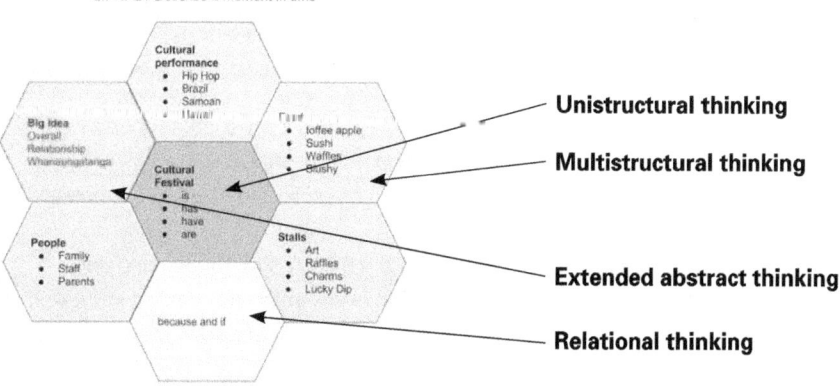

Figure 4.7: Description of a cultural festival, based on SOLO hexagon plan in Figure 4.6

The cultural festival is an a event that Newmarket primary school celebrates.

The cultural festival has food such as taro, sushi and waffles. Food is important because if there weren't any food people will be hungry and they will go home early.

The cultural festival has stalls such as Clay charms, Raffles and lucky dip. Stalls are important because if there weren't any stalls we wouldn't get any money for our school and show our art.

The cultural festival has people such as family, cousins and staff. People are important because if there weren't people there it wouldn't really be an a event.

The cultural festival has cultural dances from children such as Hip Hop, Samoan and Indian. The cultural performance is important because if there weren't any performances it wouldn't really be a cultural event.

Overall the purpose of the cultural festival is to bring everyone together at Newmarket primary school and build Whanaungatanga which is about building relationships. I believe whanaungatanga is important at Newmarket school because people are important because if there weren't any people we wouldn't have a school.

Overall I believe this writing is at extended abstract because I can list 3 or more ideas and can link my ideas by using words such as, if and because. I can include an overall statement and put a big Idea at the end of my writing.

I think R____'s writing is at Extended abstract because she used 3 or more linking ideas using words, such as, because and if. She has included the purpose and an overall statement. I think R____ has to work on spaces between her paragraphs. - By E____

Text patterns for connecting ideas (relational task)

Language function: Connecting ideas (relational task) – deep or higher-order thinking
Language functions that help ELLs connect ideas include tasks using academic verbs such as *sequence, classify, compare and contrast, explain causes, explain effects, analyse, form an analogy*.

Language structure: Connected ideas
Language structures that help ELLs connect ideas include sentence starters and sentence frames, key words and appropriate grammar (see Tables 4.3 and 4.6).

This subsection focuses on the tasks of *sequencing* and *comparing and contrasting* to illustrate how SOLO strategies such as SOLO maps, as visual summaries of text patterns for linking ideas, can support these tasks.

Sequencing with SOLO strategies

Sequencing is part of the thinking strategies students use every day: from sequencing movements in kicking a ball or riding a scooter, to sequencing sounds in speech, letters in writing or symbols in maths operations, to sequencing technology-related actions in using an iPad or programming in Scratch MIT. Students who struggle with sequencing will struggle in pre-reading, comprehension, writing, thinking mathematically and any other academic activity. It is therefore important to give ELLs a strong foundation in the function and structure of the academic language of sequencing.

Students may need explicit support when predicting the next step in a sequence, creating a sequence, recognising sequential patterns and making decisions on next steps based on sequences. Some helpful supports are:
- video or still digital images (Figure 4.8) and sentence frames (Table 4.3) to help ELLs recall the steps in a process when describing and sequencing
- programming in Scratch MIT (https://scratch.mit.edu) to help ELLs understand the patterns of sequencing and practise using the language of sequencing when they explain the steps in their programming to others (Figure 4.9)
- the HOT SOLO sequence map (Exhibit 4.3), which can be used to help students describe a process, write a report or a recount or give an oral account.

Figure 4.8: Using a camera (video or still) to recall the steps in a process

Description & Sequencing

Use a camera for recalling ideas.

Table 4.3: Supporting language structures for a sequencing task

Function: Sequence	**Question:** What is the order?	
Sentence starters and sentence frames	**Key words**	**Grammar**
first ... second ... third ... generally ... furthermore ... finally in the first place ... also ... lastly The first thing that happened was ... After that ... The next event was ... Earlier in the day ... Immediately following that ... First I ... , second I ... and finally I .... First we ... , later we ... . In the beginning I ... , but at the end I ... . During ... I ... while we ... . First ... , then ... and finally ... First ..., afterward ..., and subsequently ... Earlier today I ... later I ... First ..., second ..., then ..., eventually ...	first, second, finally, the first point is, lastly, the following, first of all, at first, at the beginning, then, next, after, afterwards, before, when, while, during, soon, prior to, immediately, once, suddenly, as soon as, eventually, in the end, at last, to begin with, until	Word order

Figure 4.9: ELL's program in Scratch MIT, reinforcing the patterns of sequencing

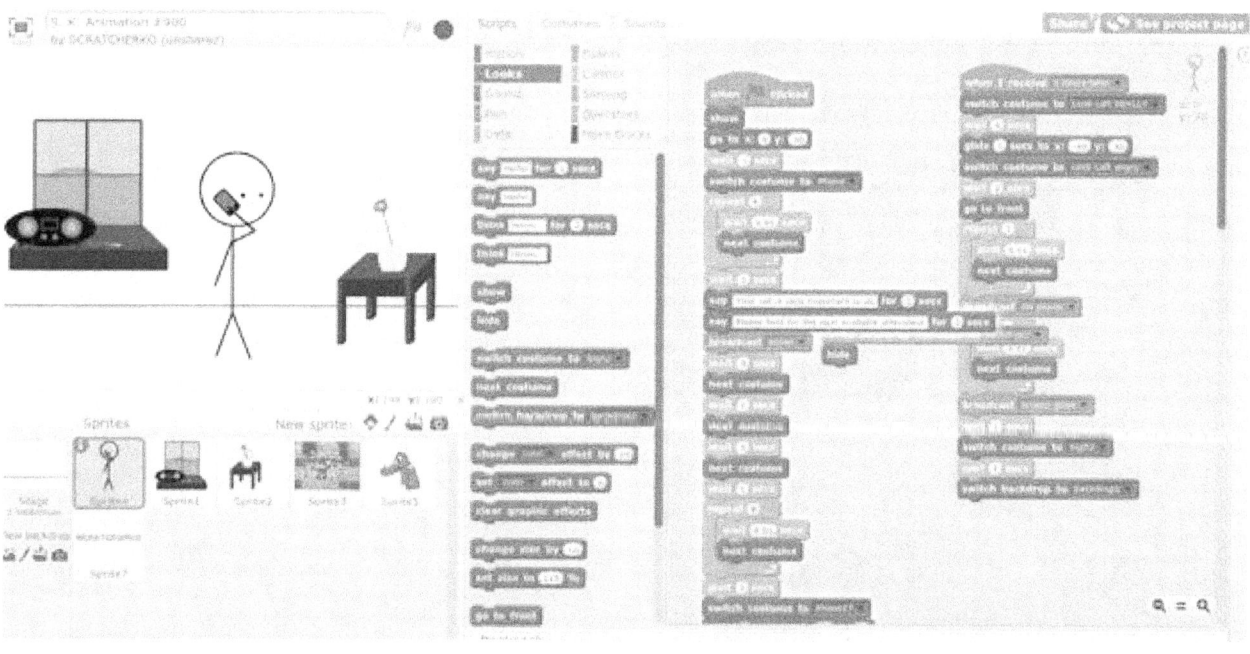

Exhibit 4.3: HOT SOLO Sequence map as a relational supporting strategy

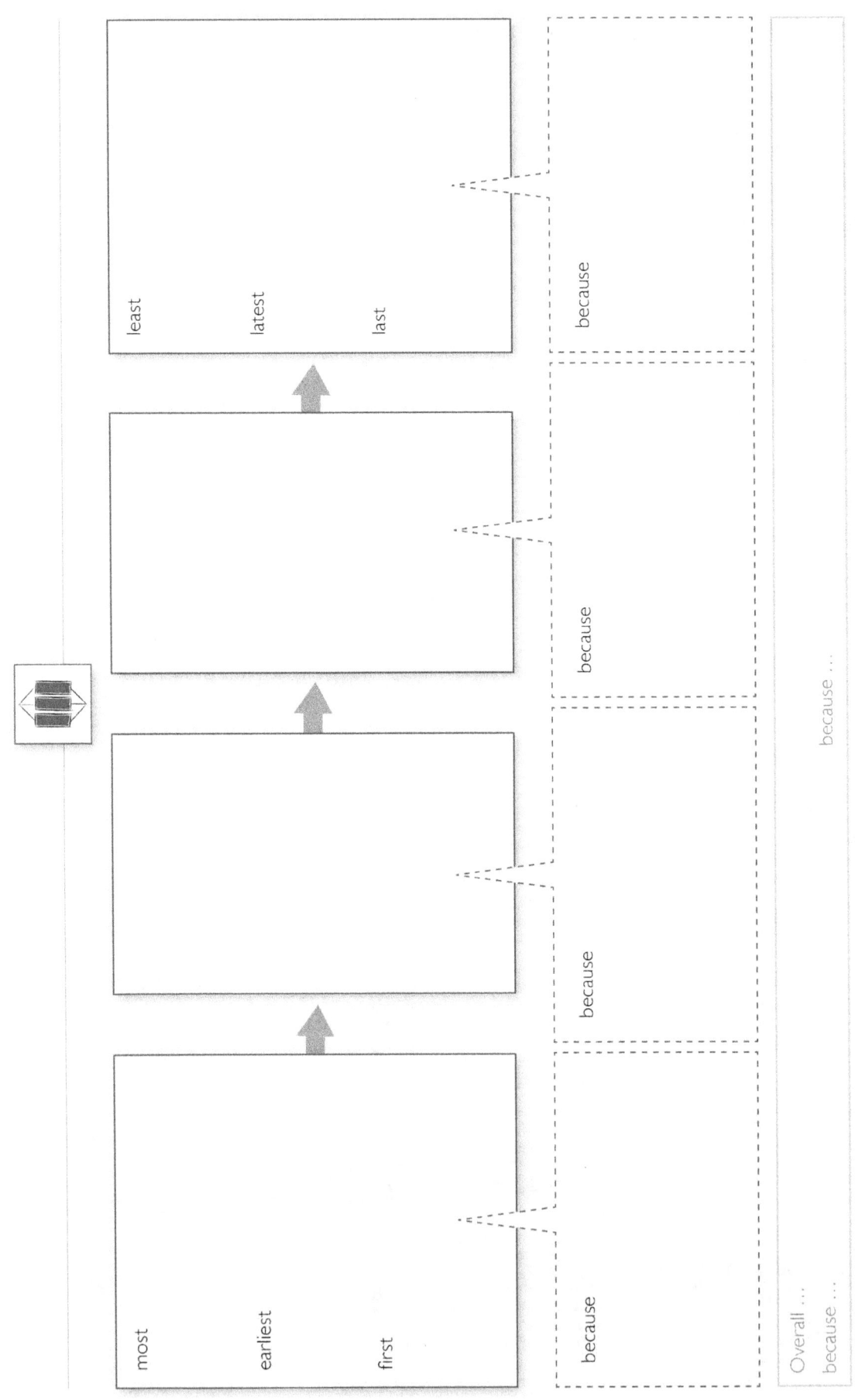

© *Hooked-on-Thinking. Pam Hook and Julie Mills, 2011. All rights reserved.*

Exhibit 4.4 presents a HOT SOLO Sequence self-assessment rubric, which the teacher and ELL can use to identify the SOLO level of the ELL's sequencing work. You can see an example of how to apply this approach in Table 4.4, which gives examples of ELL work, along with effective prompts, at each SOLO level.

A range of examples of ELLs' sequencing work then follows.

Exhibit 4.4: HOT SOLO Sequence self-assessment rubric for SOLO-differentiated outcomes

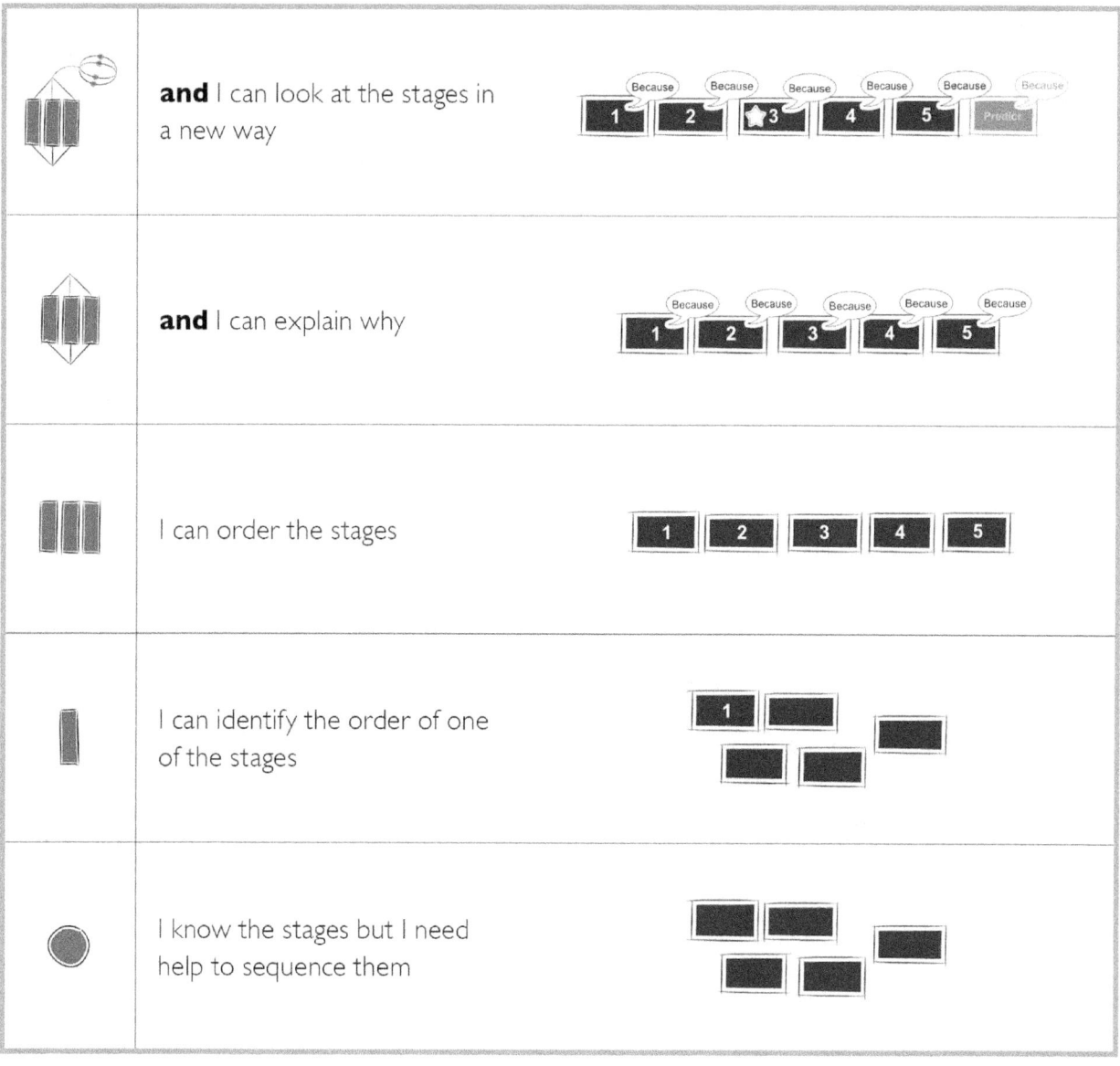

SOLO learning log

My sequencing statement is at a _____ SOLO level outcome because ...

My next step is to ...

© *Hooked-on-Thinking. Pam Hook and Julie Mills, 2011. All rights reserved.*

Table 4.4: Applying the HOT SOLO Sequence self-assessment rubric to ELL sequencing work

SOLO level	Learning outcome	Effective prompts	Example of ELL work at this level
Prestructural	The student points or draws. **(Preproduction)**	Show me …	
Unistructural	The student identifies the position of an object, event, place or person in the sequence. **(Early production)**	What is first?	first wash hands
Multistructural	The student identifies the position/order of several objects, events, places or people in the sequence … **(Speech emergence)**	What happened next?	First wash your hands. Next make the biscuits. Then cook them.
Relational	… **and** the student explains the order of different objects, events, places or people in the sequence (using *because/so that*). **(Intermediate fluency)**	Why did it happen like this?	First wash your hands *because* they are dirty. Next make the biscuits. Then cook them so you can eat them.
Extended abstract	… **and** the student is able to make a claim or prediction about the overall sequence (double *because* structure). **(Advanced fluency)**	What might happen next?	[Same as relational plus …] Taking orders to make more biscuits *because* people loved how they tasted *because* we were careful to follow the recipe.

Examples of ELL sequencing work using SOLO strategies

The following examples demonstrate:

- using images in a sequence sentence frame (Figure 4.10)
- a student's recount writing, based on a plan made using a SOLO Sequence map (Figure 4.11)
- a student's sequencing with process mapping to show what happened when the fire alarm went off (Figure 4.12)
- how ELLs work with SOLO display strips and images to sequence events in a cultural festival (Figure 4.13), typical responses at each SOLO level to sequencing prompts (Table 4.5) and a piece of writing sequencing the events of the cultural festival and using SOLO highlighting (Figure 4.14).

For an example of an oral sequence using video, go to YouTube to view "Learn how to skip" (https://youtu.be/9MafrD65MhU).

Figure 4.10: Using images in a sequence sentence frame to describe when Matariki is coming

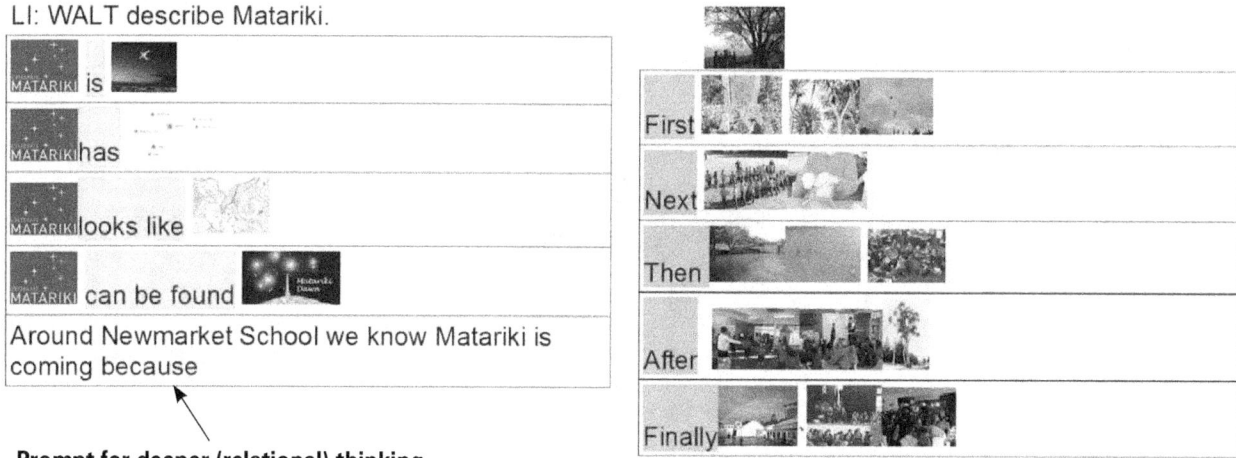

Prompt for deeper (relational) thinking

Figure 4.11: Sequencing in recount writing, based on a SOLO Sequence map

When I went back to school I saw builders all around. First they used a jackhammer to break the wall. Then we went into Mrs Van Schaijik's room and it was dirt all inside and it was muddy and it was all broken. I saw a saw cut the wood for the walls. Next we got back to the front of the school and saw a big skip full of rubbish. I felt bored because I had to walk around. Finally I went back to my class.

Year 3 Sample
LI: WALT plan a recount
SC: We know we are successful when we can............
- Plan our recount and use time words
- Tick the words we used in our writing
- Read our recount

Figure 4.12: Sequencing with process mapping to show what happened when the fire alarm went off

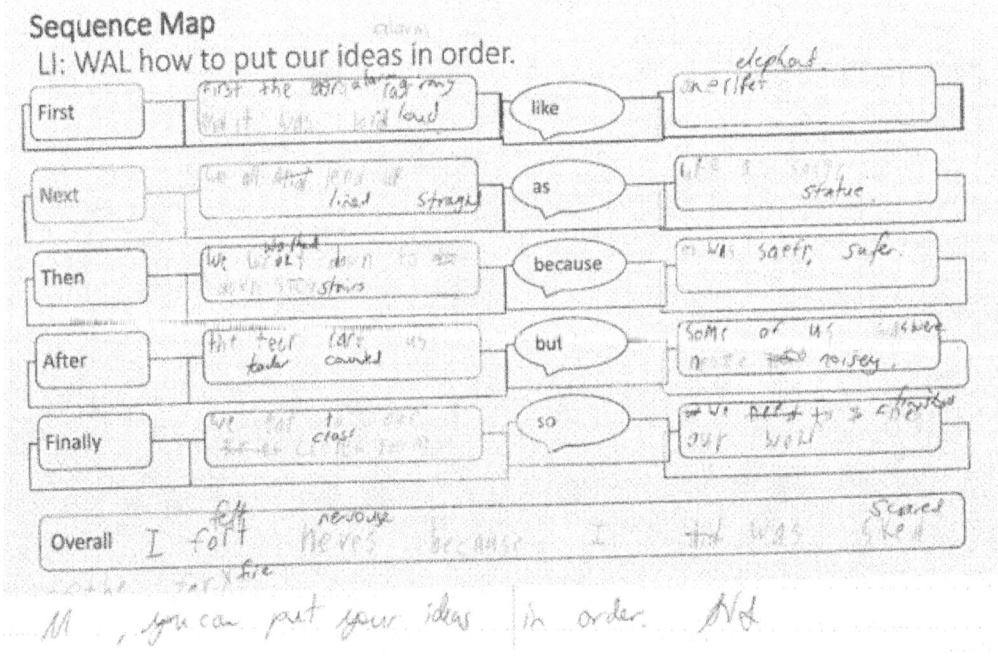

Figure 4.13: ELLs work with SOLO display strips and images to sequence events in a cultural festival

Table 4.5: Sequencing events in a cultural festival in response to prompts at each SOLO level

SOLO level	Effective prompt	ELL response
Prestructural	Show me …	
Unistructural	What is first?	We visited the classrooms and brought some art and some lunch from different countries.
Multistructural	What happened next?	We changed into our cultural costumes.
Relational	Why did it happen like this?	We performed for our parents and our school community.
Extended abstract	What might happen next?	We felt proud because we shared our performance at our school cultural festival.

Figure 4.14: Sequencing writing about a cultural festival with SOLO highlighting

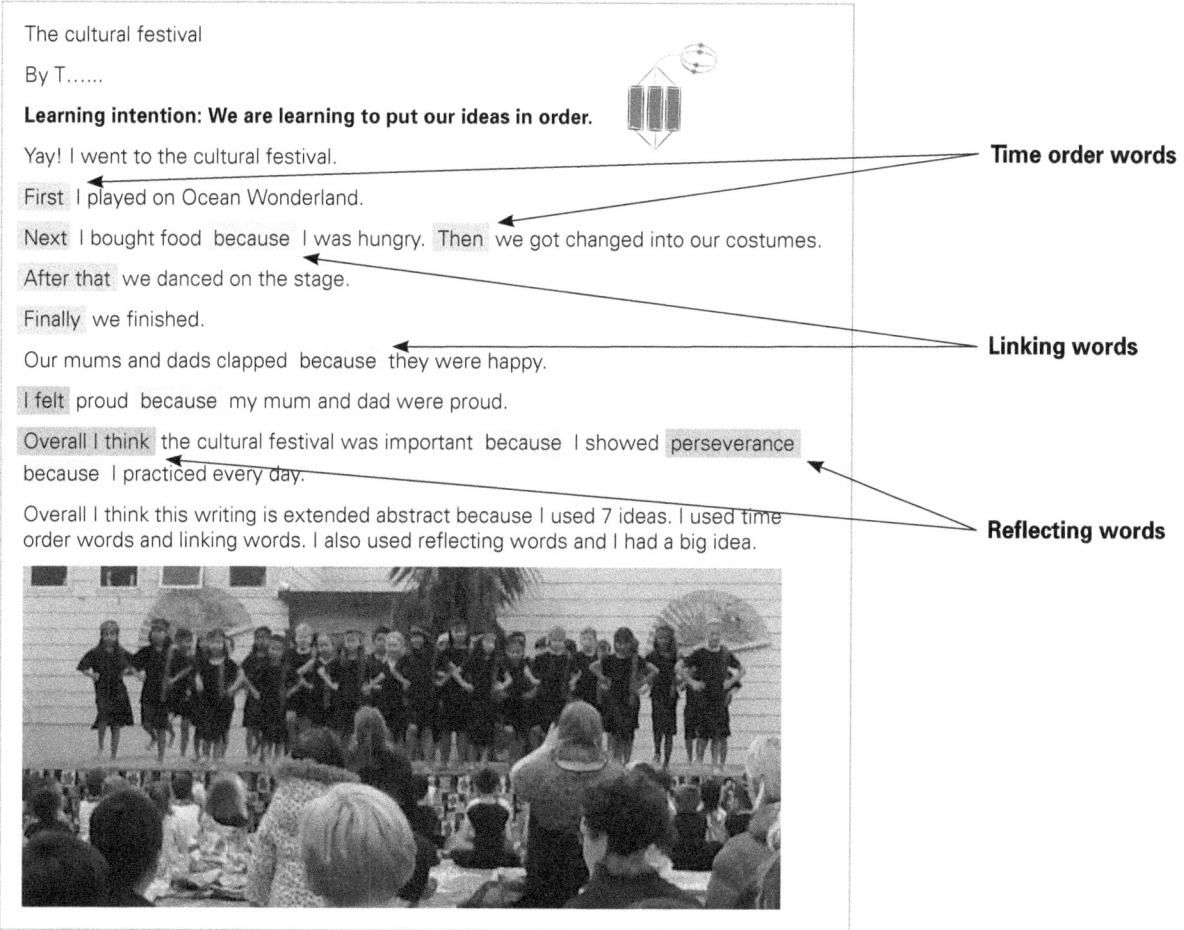

Comparing and contrasting with SOLO strategies

The compare and contrast text pattern extends the focus of a task from organising on the basis of similarities to organising on the basis of similarities and differences. Language structures (Table 4.6) and a HOT SOLO Compare and Contrast map (Exhibit 4.5) can support ELLs when they undertake a compare and contrast task.

Exhibit 4.6 presents a HOT SOLO Compare and Contrast self-assessment rubric, which the teacher and ELL can use to identify the SOLO level of the ELL's compare and contrast work. You can see an example of how to apply this approach in Table 4.7, which gives examples of ELL work, along with effective prompts, at each SOLO level.

A range of examples of ELLs' compare and contrast work then follows.

Table 4.6: Supporting language structures for a compare and contrast task

Function: Compare and contrast	**Questions:** How is it similar? How is it different?	
Sentence starters and sentence frames	**Key words**	**Grammar**
Both X and Y have … X is similar to Y in that (they) … X and Y are similar in that (they) … Like X, Y [verb] … In like manner, One way in which X is similar to Y is (that) … Another way in which X is similar to Y is (that) …	like, similar to, also, unlike, similarly, in the same way, likewise, again, compared with, in contrast, in like manner, contrasted with, on the contrary, however, although, yet, even though, still, but, nevertheless, conversely, at the same time, regardless, despite, while, on the one hand … on the other hand	Use conjunctions, transitional adverbs and/or phrases. Transitional adverb goes between separate sentences. Word order: Conjunction + subject + verb, subject + verb Subject + verb + conjunction + subject + verb…

Exhibit 4.5: HOT SOLO Compare and Contrast map as a relational supporting strategy

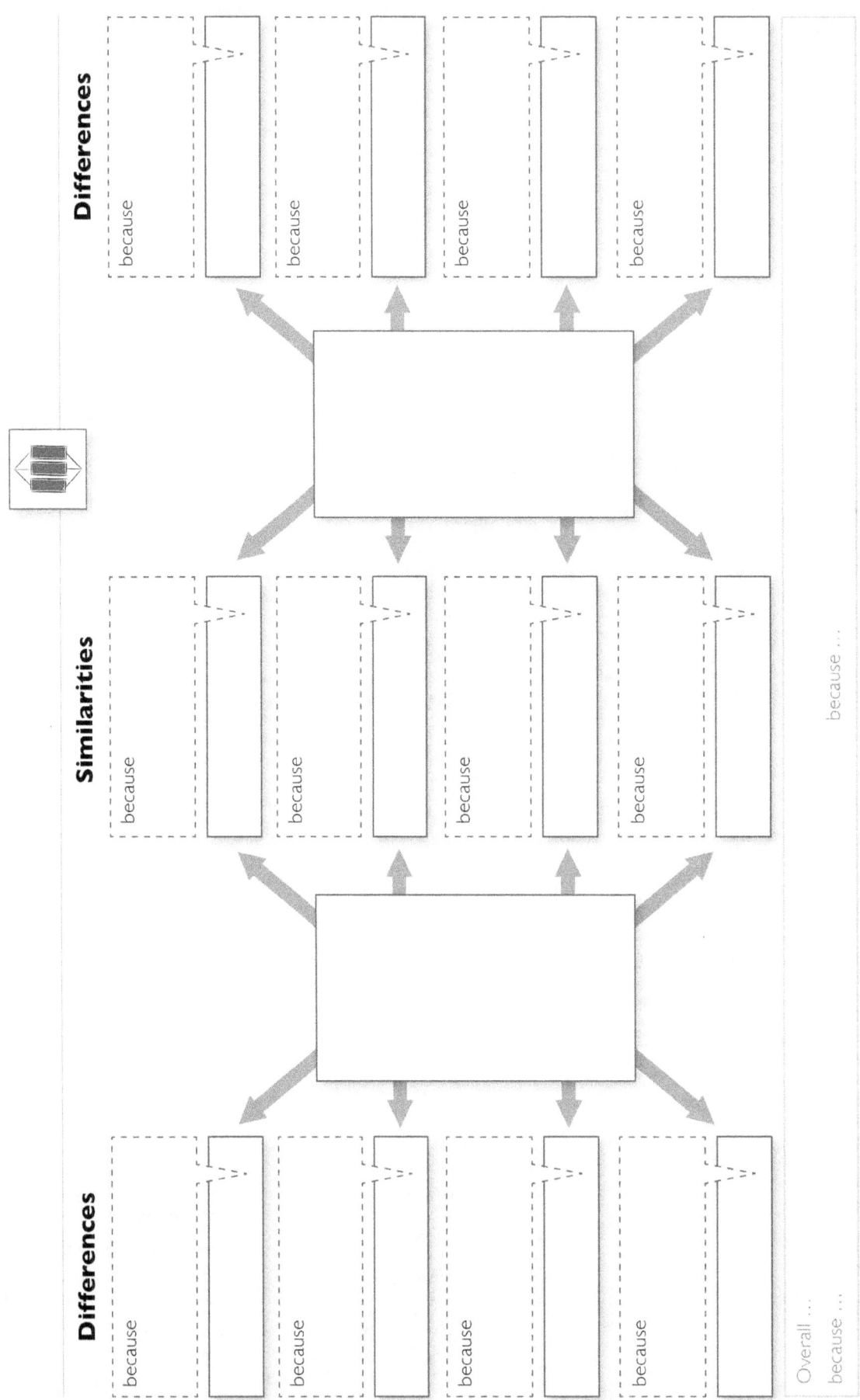

© *Hooked-on-Thinking. Pam Hook and Julie Mills, 2011. All rights reserved.*

Exhibit 4.6: HOT SOLO Compare and Contrast self-assessment rubric for SOLO-differentiated outcomes

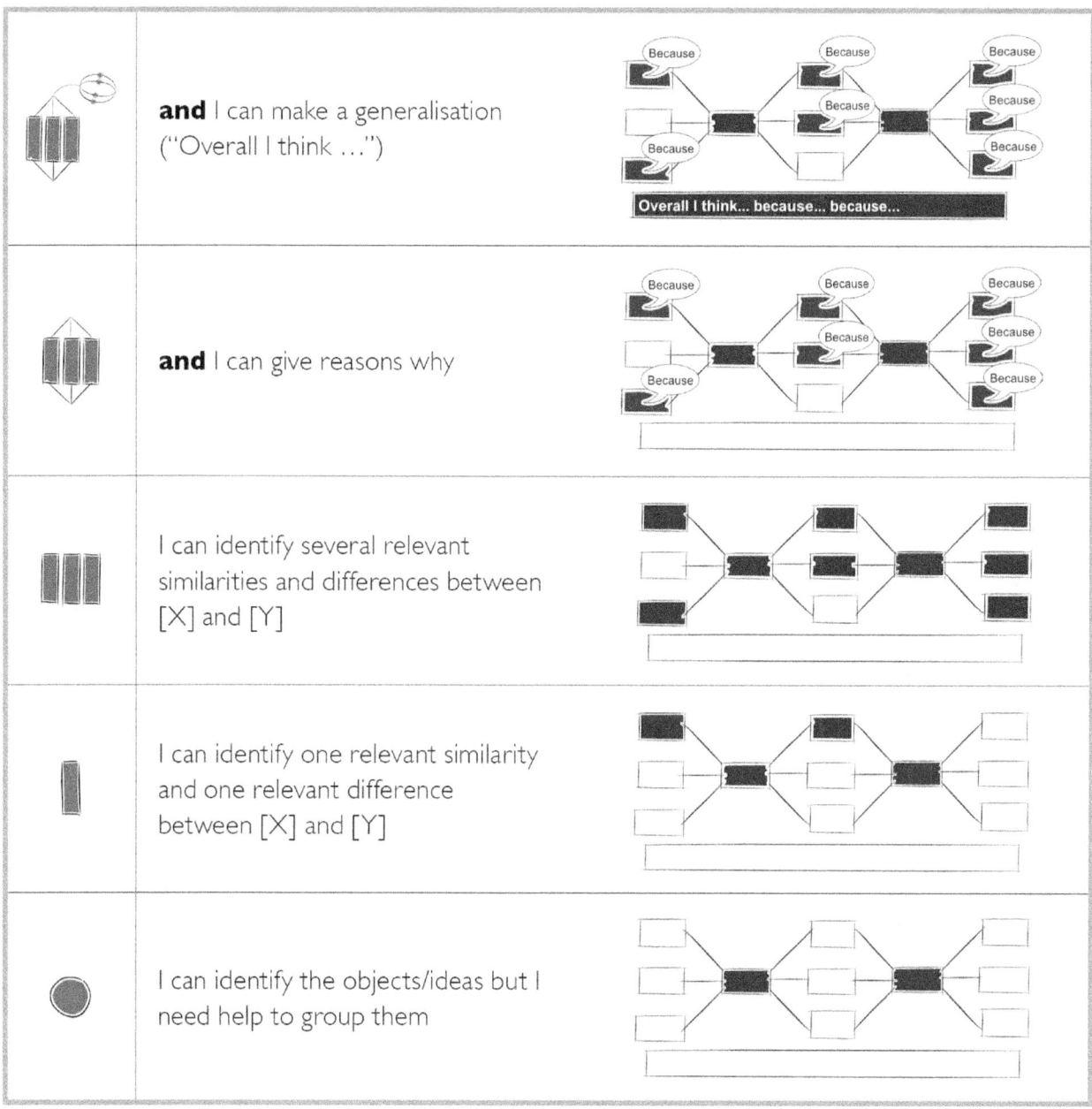

SOLO learning log

My comparison is at a _____ SOLO level outcome because …

My next step is to …

© *Hooked-on-Thinking. Pam Hook and Julie Mills, 2011. All rights reserved.*

Table 4.7: Applying the HOT SOLO Compare and Contrast self-assessment rubric to ELL work that compares and contrasts dogs and cats

SOLO level	Learning outcome	Effective prompts	Example of ELL work at this level
Prestructural	The student points or draws. **(Preproduction)**	Draw thing 1 and thing 2.	
Unistructural	The student identifies a similarity or a difference. **(Early production)**	What is the same?	They both have fur.
Multistructural	The student identifies several similarities and differences ... **(Speech emergence)**	List the similarities and differences.	They both have fur but the dog is bigger than the cat.
Relational	... **and** the student explains reasons behind the similarities and differences (using *because*) ... **(Intermediate fluency).**	Why are they similar? Why are they different?	They both have fur *because* they are both mammals. However, the dog is bigger than the cat *because* Labradors are a big dog breed.
Extended abstract	... **and** the student is able to make a claim about the extent of the similarities or differences between the two (double *because* structure). **(Advanced fluency)**	Are they more similar than they are different? Why or why not?	[Same as relational plus ...] Overall I think a dog and a cat are more similar than they are different *because* they both have to fit into our lives in similar ways *because* they are household pets.

Examples of ELL compare and contrast work using SOLO strategies

The following examples demonstrate:
- a writing plan using a HOT SOLO Compare and Contrast map (Figure 4.15) and the resulting piece of writing that compares and contrasts cars and scooters and that includes the student's reflection on this writing (Figure 4.16)
- a SOLO Compare and Contrast map a nine-year-old created using Google Drawings to help scaffold her writing in which she compared and contrasted her performance experience in two dances (Figure 4.17). She chose to adapt the map by placing photos for comparison outside the map so the detail is easier to observe.

Figure 4.15: Using a HOT SOLO Compare and Contrast map to plan to compare and contrast cars and scooters

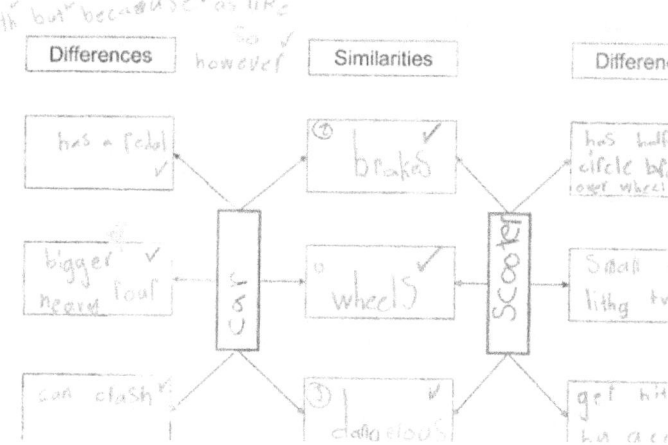

Figure 4.16: Comparing and contrasting a car and a scooter, based on a plan made with the SOLO Compare and Contrast map in Figure 4.15

> Learning intention: We are learning to compare a car and a scooter.
>
> Success criteria: I know I'm successful when I use relational thinking such as *both, but, because*. When I compare a car and scooter I can use words like *different* and *same*.
>
> Both cars and scooters are vehicles that take you to school. Cars can take you to far places but scooters can only take you short distances. Both vehicles have wheels. But scooters only have two small, light wheels and sometimes three and cars have four big, heavy wheels.
>
> Both vehicles need to have brakes for safety just in case they are going to crash. But car brakes are foot pedals and scooter brakes are a half circle over the back wheel. They both need a foot to make them work.
>
> Both vehicles can be dangerous because a car can crash into another car and scooters can be hit by a car.
>
> I believe both vehicles are the same because they both take you to school but scooters are different because it takes more time. However scooters don't pollute but help the environment. Cars are different because they hurt the environment by making gas. I would still choose a car to go to school because my parents have to leave early and it's quicker to get to places.
>
> **Reflection**
>
> I beilivie this writing is extended abstract because I used 3 of those ideas about transport. I used linking words to link my ideas to this writing and I summeriz my ideas using an I belivie sentence. My next step is to keep working on my capital letters and fullstops.

Figure 4.17: SOLO Compare and Contrast map a student created using Google Drawings to compare and contrast two dances

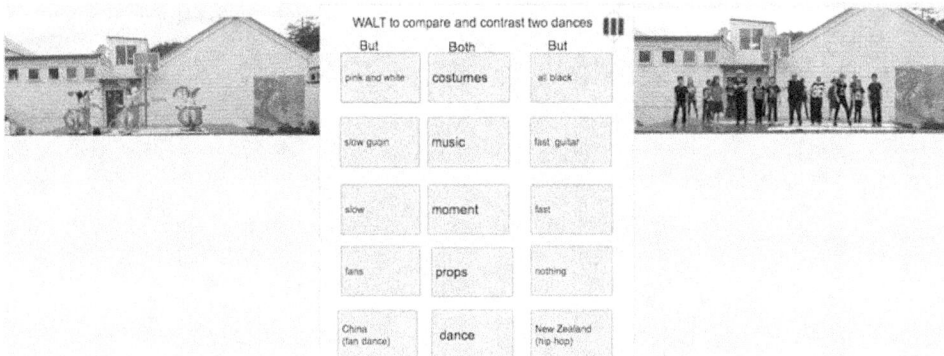

Text patterns for extending ideas (extended abstract task)

Language function: Extending ideas (SOLO extended abstract task) – conceptual or higher-order thinking
Language functions that help ELLs extend ideas include tasks using academic verbs such as *generalise, predict, evaluate, hypothesise* and *create*.

Language structures: Extended ideas
Language structures that help ELLs extend ideas include sentence starters and sentence frames, key words and appropriate grammar (as in Table 4.8).

This subsection focuses on the task of *describing, explaining and generalising* to illustrate how SOLO strategies such as SOLO maps, as visual summaries of text patterns for extending ideas, can support this task.

Describing, explaining and generalising with SOLO strategies

The HookED SOLO Describe++ map (Exhibit 4.7) extends the text pattern of description (gathering information about the relevant attributes) to include patterns for explaining causes and then making a generalisation. It supports surface, deep and conceptual (higher-order) thinking and encourages use of simple sentences and complex sentences and paragraphing in oral and written language.

It is also possible to use the HookED SOLO Describe++ strip (Exhibit 4.8), a cut-down version of the map, which is a useful prompt for oral language or early written language. It prompts thinking at each SOLO level by asking:
- What do you notice? (unistructural and multistructural)
- Why do you think it is like that? (relational)
- What does it make you wonder? (extended abstract)

Exhibit 4.9 presents a HookED SOLO Describe++ self-assessment rubric, which the teacher and ELL can use to identify the SOLO level of the ELL's description, explanation and generalisation. You can see an example of how to apply this approach in Table 4.9, which gives examples of ELL writing, along with effective prompts, at each SOLO level.

A range of examples of ELLs' work to describe, explain and generalise then follows.

Table 4.8: Supporting language structures for describing, explaining and generalising

Function: Describe, explain and generalise	**Questions:** • What can you see? Why do you think it is like that? What does it make you wonder? • What can you see? Why do you think it is like that? How effective is it?	
Sentence starters and sentence frames	**Key words**	**Grammar**
I notice ... I think it is like that because ... It makes me wonder ... I notice ... I think this means that ... An exception might be ...	because, so that, overall, in summary, on reflection, in my opinion	Prepositional phrases

Exhibit 4.7: HookED SOLO Describe++ map

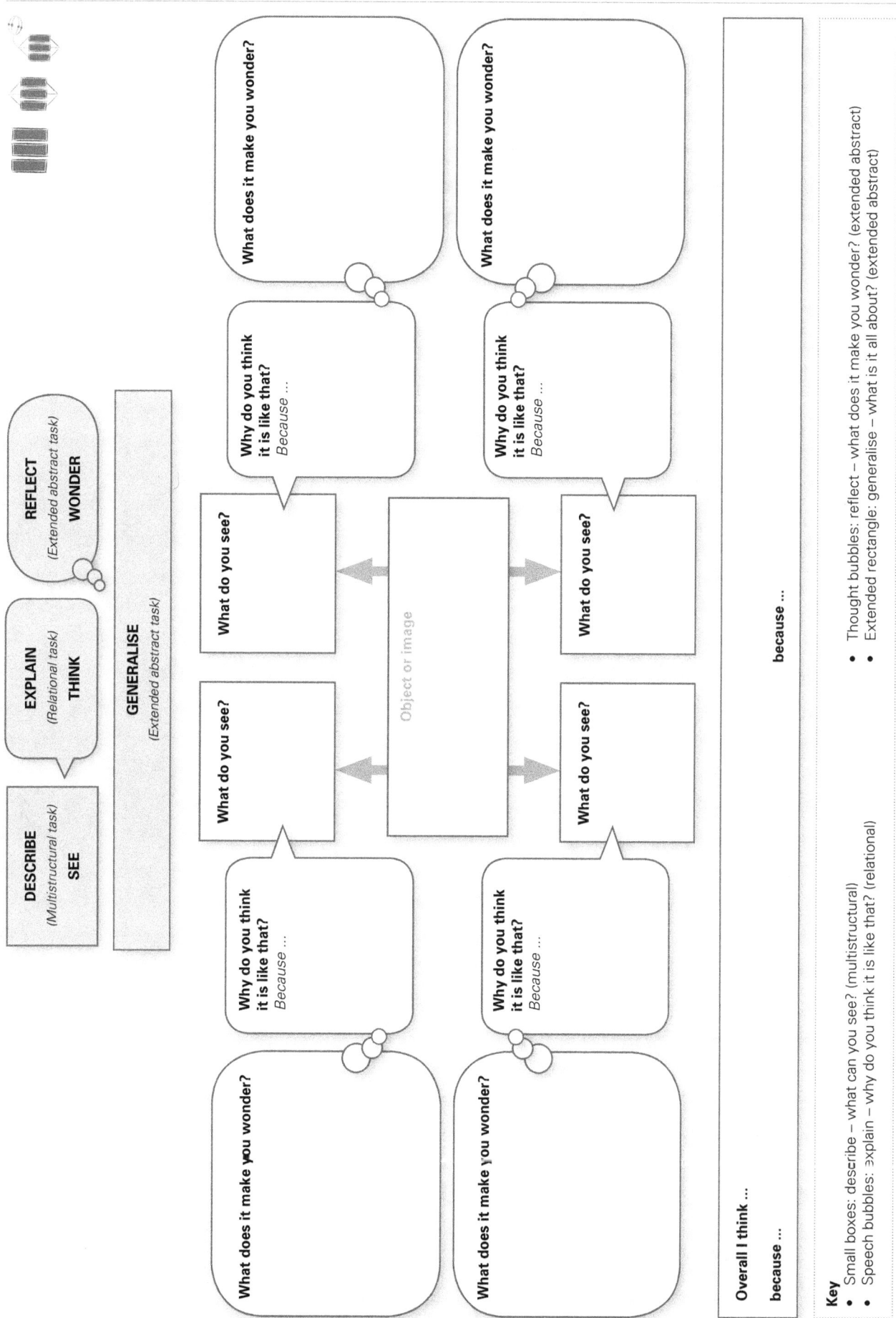

© HookED, Pam Hook, 2016. All rights reserved.

63

Exhibit 4.8: HookED SOLO Describe++ strip

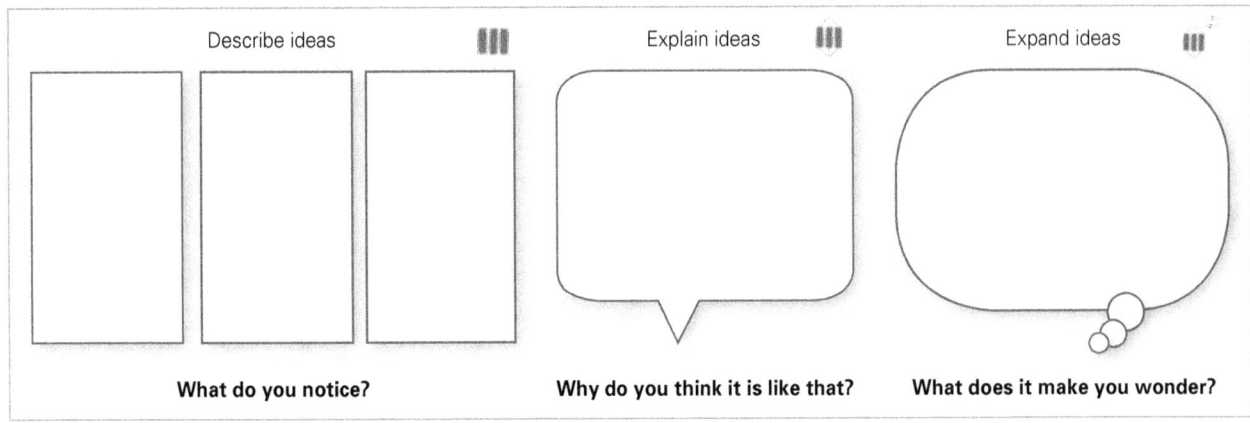

Describe ideas — What do you notice?

Explain ideas — Why do you think it is like that?

Expand ideas — What does it make you wonder?

© HookED. Pam Hook 2016. All rights reserved.

Exhibit 4.9: HookED SOLO Describe++ self-assessment rubric

SOLO level		Learning outcome
Extended abstract 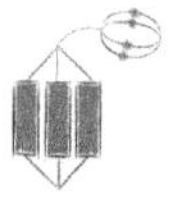	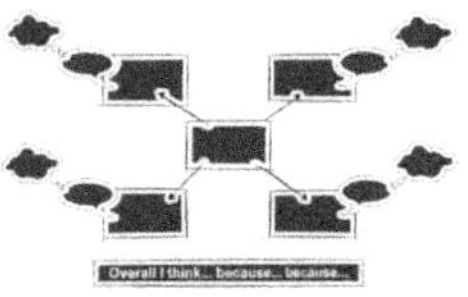	My description identifies several relevant features, links these and makes a generalisation. It integrates these generalisations into a new understanding.
Relational 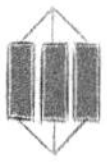	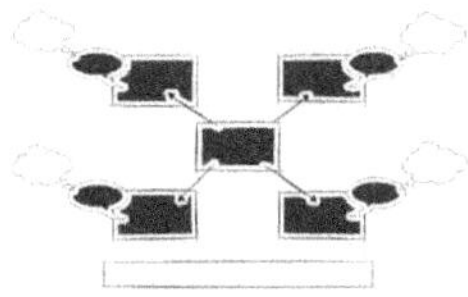	My description identifies several relevant features and links these by explanation.
Multistructural 	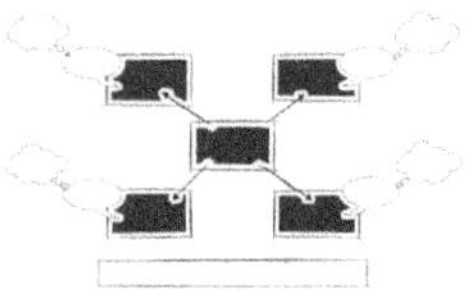	My description identifies several relevant features.
Unistructural 	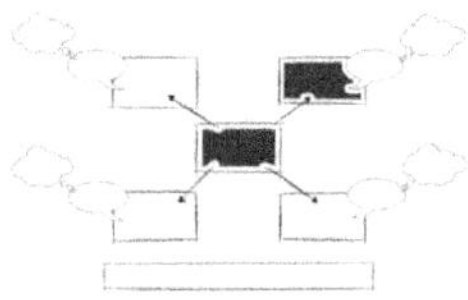	My description identifies one relevant feature.
Prestructural	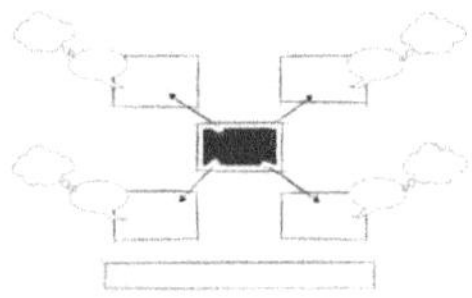	I need help to identify any relevant features.

My learning outcome is _____ because _____

My next step is to _____

© HookED. Pam Hook, 2013. All rights reserved.

64

Table 4.9: Applying the HookED SOLO Describe++ self-assessment rubric to ELL work that describes, explains and generalises about chopsticks

SOLO level	Learning outcome	Example of ELL work at this level
Prestructural	The student points or draws. **(Preproduction)**	
Unistructural	The student identifies one attribute. **(Early production)**	pair of chopsticks
Multistructural	The student identifies several attributes of the whole ... **(Speech emergence)**	On the table I see a pair of chopsticks and a bowl of instant noodles.
Relational	... and the student explains why they think the attribute is like it is ... **(Intermediate fluency).**	*[Same as multistructural plus ...]* I think the chopsticks are for picking up the noodles. I think the bowl is to hold the noodles in one place.
Extended abstract	... and the student reflects on the attributes individually and collectively. **(Advanced fluency)**	*[Same as relational plus ...]* I wonder how they will use the chopsticks to get the liquid around the noodles. I wonder if it would be easier to pick up the noodles if they were in an even smaller container like a cup. Overall I wonder what role the food available in any country has on the utensils developed to eat with.

Examples of ELL work to describe, explain and generalise using SOLO strategies

The following examples demonstrate:
- an ELL's use of a cut-down HookED SOLO Describe++ map to describe, explain and wonder about an ambulance using a "See think wonder" routine (Figure 4.18)
- collaborative writing using a cut-down HookED SOLO Describe++ map to describe, explain and wonder about a butterfly (Figure 4.19)
- use of the full HookED SOLO Describe++ map, where the prompts are the same but the students can explore any number of observations or attributes, to help six- and seven-year-old ELLs to plan writing that describes, explains and wonders about a kiwifruit (Figure 4.20)
- a sample of writing based on the plan shown in Figure 4.20 (Figure 4.21).

Figure 4.18: Using a HookED SOLO Describe++ strip to describe, explain and wonder about an ambulance

Figure 4.19: Using a HookED SOLO Describe++ strip in collaborative writing to describe, explain and wonder about a butterfly

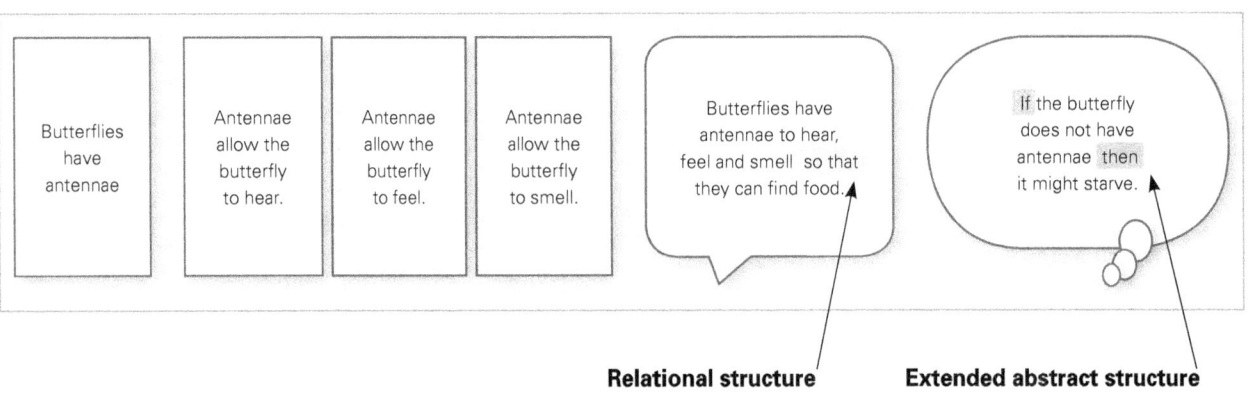

Figure 4.20: Using a full HookED SOLO Describe++ map as a plan for writing a description of a kiwifruit

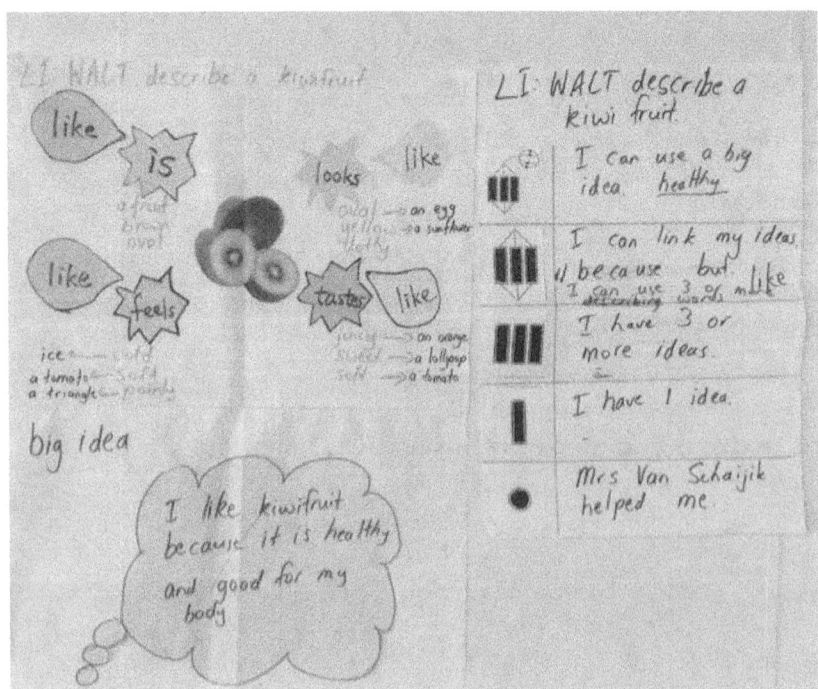

Table 4.9: Applying the HookED SOLO Describe++ self-assessment rubric to ELL work that describes, explains and generalises about chopsticks

SOLO level	Learning outcome	Example of ELL work at this level
Prestructural	The student points or draws. **(Preproduction)**	
Unistructural	The student identifies one attribute. **(Early production)**	pair of chopsticks
Multistructural	The student identifies several attributes of the whole … **(Speech emergence)**	On the table I see a pair of chopsticks and a bowl of instant noodles.
Relational	… and the student explains why they think the attribute is like it is … **(Intermediate fluency).**	[Same as multistructural plus …] I think the chopsticks are for picking up the noodles. I think the bowl is to hold the noodles in one place.
Extended abstract	… and the student reflects on the attributes individually and collectively. **(Advanced fluency)**	[Same as relational plus …] I wonder how they will use the chopsticks to get the liquid around the noodles. I wonder if it would be easier to pick up the noodles if they were in an even smaller container like a cup. Overall I wonder what role the food available in any country has on the utensils developed to eat with.

Examples of ELL work to describe, explain and generalise using SOLO strategies

The following examples demonstrate:
- an ELL's use of a cut-down HookED SOLO Describe++ map to describe, explain and wonder about an ambulance using a "See think wonder" routine (Figure 4.18)
- collaborative writing using a cut-down HookED SOLO Describe++ map to describe, explain and wonder about a butterfly (Figure 4.19)
- use of the full HookED SOLO Describe++ map, where the prompts are the same but the students can explore any number of observations or attributes, to help six- and seven-year-old ELLs to plan writing that describes, explains and wonders about a kiwifruit (Figure 4.20)
- a sample of writing based on the plan shown in Figure 4.20 (Figure 4.21).

Figure 4.18: Using a HookED SOLO Describe++ strip to describe, explain and wonder about an ambulance

Figure 4.19: Using a HookED SOLO Describe++ strip in collaborative writing to describe, explain and wonder about a butterfly

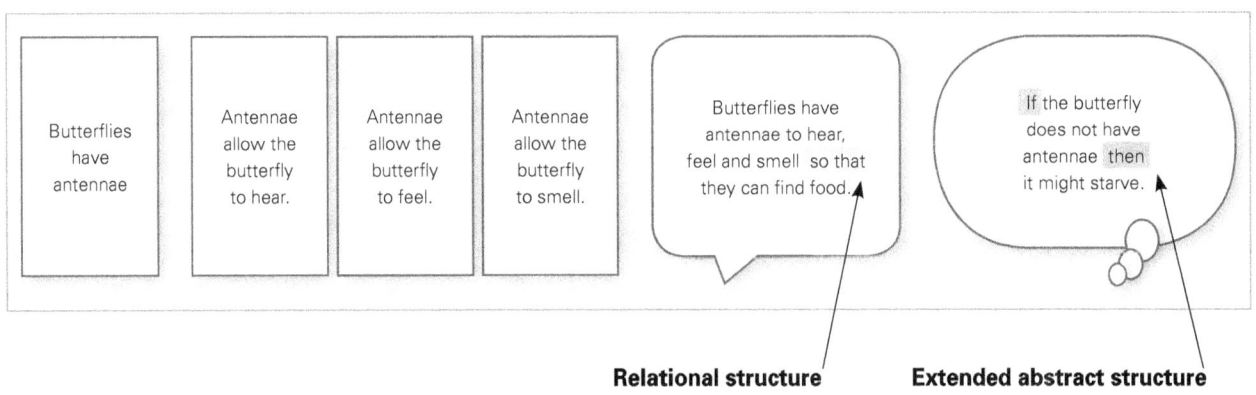

Figure 4.20: Using a full HookED SOLO Describe++ map as a plan for writing a description of a kiwifruit

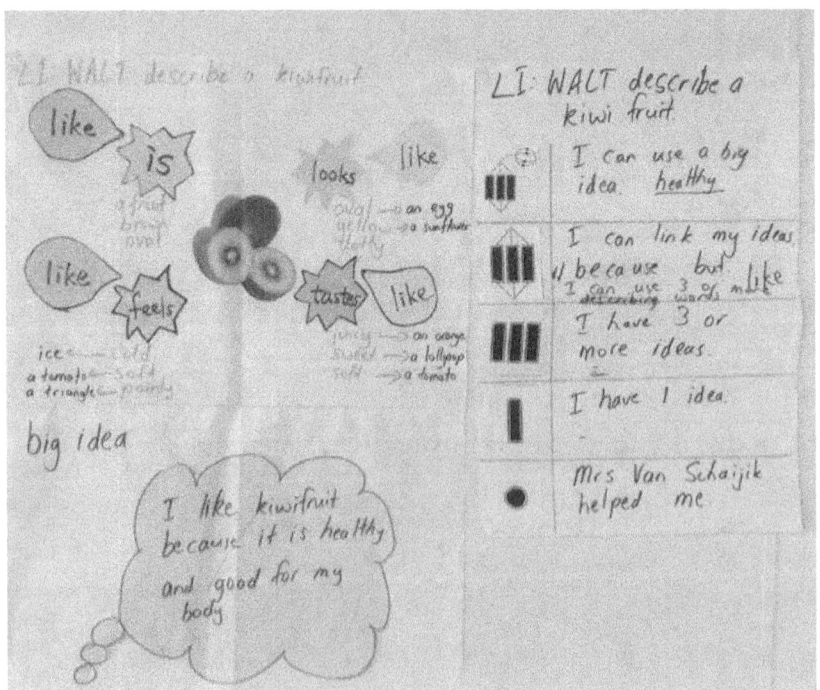

Figure 4.21: Describing, explaining and generalising about a kiwifruit, based on a plan made with the SOLO Describe++ map in Figure 4.20

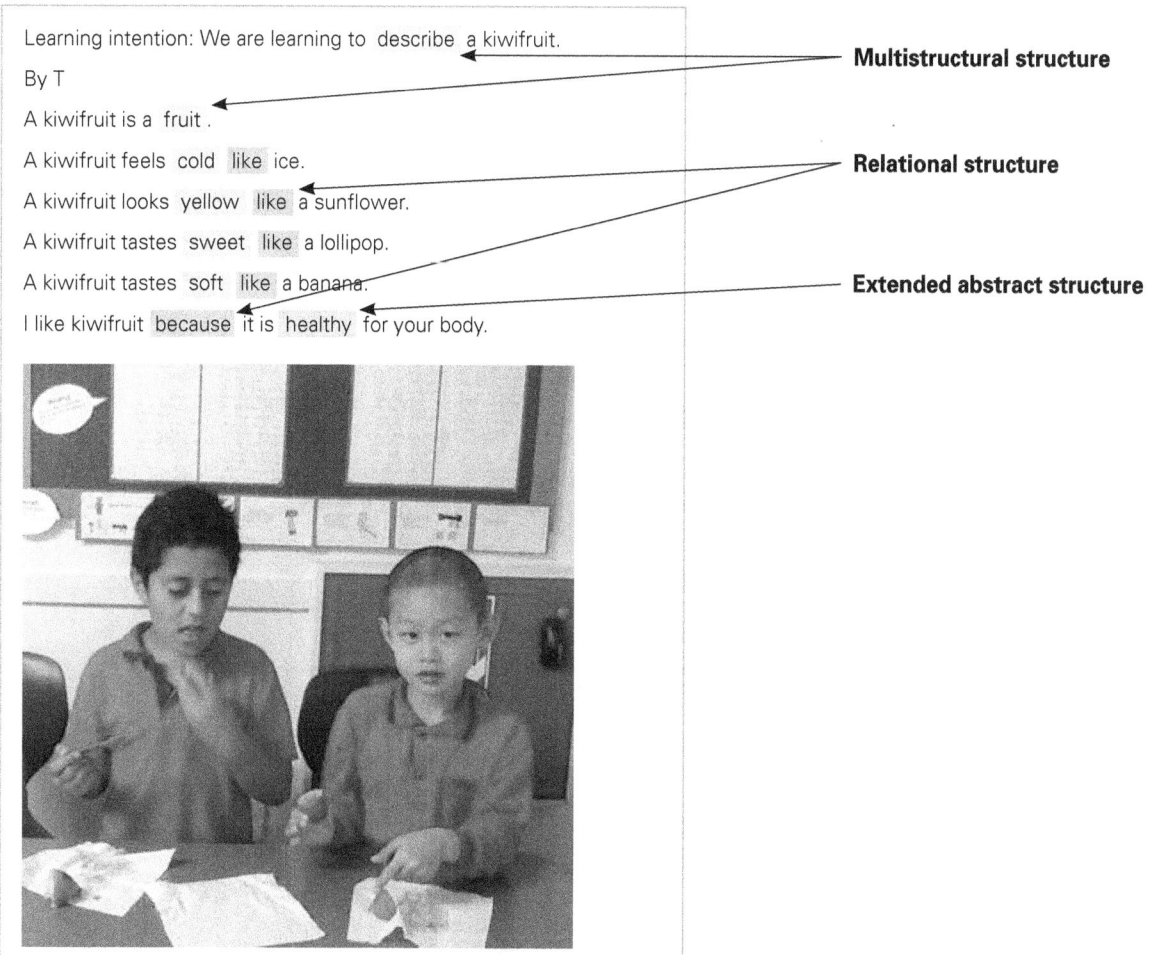

Learning intention: We are learning to describe a kiwifruit. ← **Multistructural structure**

By T

A kiwifruit is a fruit.

A kiwifruit feels cold like ice.

A kiwifruit looks yellow like a sunflower. ← **Relational structure**

A kiwifruit tastes sweet like a lollipop.

A kiwifruit tastes soft like a banana. ← **Extended abstract structure**

I like kiwifruit because it is healthy for your body.

Conclusions

To encourage practitioners to have conversations about classroom contexts for L2 acquisition, we have shared the SOLO Taxonomy strategies and approaches that have been successful in helping Newmarket Primary School teachers find a balance among the teaching and learning conditions that matter most for students as they acquire L2.

The SOLO-based strategies (sentence frames, visual mapping, rubrics, hexagons etc) are simple, practical and able to be implemented by any classroom teacher. They are designed to help all teachers teach with balance – teach in ways that matter for ELLs. The strategies help teachers establish baseline measures for ELLs in their classes, plan effective next steps for learning and monitor learning outcomes so every ELL has the opportunity, support and challenge to learn academic English. They also give ELLs a model that will help them find balance when learning to learn in both L1 and L2.

Our experience affirms SOLO Taxonomy as a simple and powerful model to support ELLs in acquiring academic English. We believe that the SOLO strategies are powerful because of the simple ways in which they make the academic language of learning visible to ELLs. With SOLO, both the ELLs and their L2 teacher share a common vocabulary for learning. The teacher begins to see learning through the eyes of their students, and the students to see learning through the eyes of their teacher. Finding Brown's elusive "balance" and "feeding L2 learners words", as inspired by the Samoan proverb, are a natural consequence.

References

Alton-Lee, A. (2003). *Quality Teaching for Diverse Students in Schooling: Best evidence synthesis iteration.* Wellington: Ministry of Education.

Biggs, J. (1999). What the student does: teaching for enhanced learning. *Higher Education Research and Development* 18(1): 57–75.

Biggs, J and Tang, C. (2007). *Teaching for Quality Learning at University.* Society for Research into Higher Education.

Brown, DF. (2011). A sense of balance in English language teaching: reflections. *TESOLANZ Journal* 19: 67–73.

Cook, V. (2005). Basing teaching on the L2 user. In E Llurda (ed) *Non-native Language Teachers: Perceptions, challenges and contributions to the profession* (pp 47–61). New York: Springer.

Cummins, J. (1979). Cognitive/academic language proficiency, linguistic interdependence, the optimum age question and some other matters. *Working Papers on Bilingualism* 19: 121–129.

Cummins, J. (1994) The acquisition of English as a second language. In K Spangenberg-Urbschat and R Pritchard (eds) *Reading Instruction for ESL Students.* Delaware: International Reading Association.

Ellis, R and Shintani, N. (2013). *Exploring Language Pedagogy through Second Language Acquisition Research.* London: Routledge.

ERO. 2015. *Educationally Powerful Connections with Parents and Whānau: Executive summary and next steps.* Wellington: Education Review Office. URL: www.ero.govt.nz/National-Reports/Educationally-powerful-connections-with-parents-and-whanau-November-2015/Executive-summary-and-next-steps

Gottlieb, M. (2006). *Assessing English Language Learners: Bridges from language proficiency to academic achievement.* Thousand Oaks, CA: Corwin.

Grant, H and Dweck, CS. (2003). Clarifying achievement goals and their impact. *Journal of Personality and Social Psychology* 85(3): 541.

Gu, Y. (2013). Second language vocabulary. In J Hattie and EM Anderman (eds) *International Guide to Student Achievement* (pp 307–309). London: Routledge.

Hattie, J. (2012). *Visible Learning for Teachers: Maximizing impact on learning.* London: Routledge.

Hattie, JAC and Brown, GTL. (2004). *Cognitive Processes in asTTle: The SOLO taxonomy.* asTTle Technical Report 43. University of Auckland and Ministry of Education.

Hill, JD and Miller, KK. (2013). *Classroom Instruction that Works with English Language Learners* (2nd edn). Alexandria, VA: ASCD.

Hodgson, AM. (1992). Hexagons for systems thinking. *European Journal of Systems Dynamics* 59(1): 220–30.

Hook, P. (2015). *First Steps with SOLO Taxonomy: Applying the model in your classroom.* Invercargill: Essential Resources Educational Publishers Limited.

Hook, P and Mills, J. (2011). *SOLO Taxonomy: A Guide for Schools. Book 1. A common language of learning.* Invercargill: Essential Resources Educational Publishers Limited.

Krashen, SD and Terrell, TD. (1983). *The Natural Approach: Language acquisition in the classroom.* Hayward, CA: Alemany Press.

Le Tagaloa, AF. (1996). *O Motuga-Afa.* Alafua: Lamepa Printing Press.

Macaro, E. (2005). Codeswitching in the L2 classroom: a communication and learning strategy. In E Llurda (ed) *Non-native Language Teachers: Perceptions, challenges and contributions to the profession* (pp 63–84). New York: Springer.

May, S. (2002). Bilingualism or language loss? Pasifika communities and bilingual education. Paper presented at Ulimasao Bilingual Education Conference Alexander Park, Auckland, 3 October 2002. URL: http://ulimasao.blogspot.co.nz/p/stephen-may.html

Ministry of Education (NZ). (2008). *The English Language Learning Progressions: A resource for mainstream and ESOL teachers.* Wellington: Learning Media. URL: http://esolonline.tki.org.nz/ESOL-Online/Student-needs/English-Language-Learning-Progressions

Ministry of Education. (2009). *Ta'iala mo le Gagana Sāmoa: The Gagana Sāmoa Guidelines.* Wellington: Learning Media.

Murphy, AF. (2009). Tracking the progress of English language learners. *Phi Delta Kappan* 91(3): 25.

Reutzel, DR and Hollingsworth, PM. (1988) Highlighting key vocabulary: a generative-reciprocal procedure for teaching selected inference types. *Reading Research Quarterly* 23: 358–378.

Schleppegrell, MJ. (2012). Academic language in teaching and learning. *The Elementary School Journal* 112(3): 409–418.

Skutnabb-Kangas, T and Phillipson, R. (2008). A human rights perspective on language ecology. In A Creese, P Martin and N Hornberger (eds) *Encyclopedia of Language and Education – Volume 9: Ecology of Language* (2nd edn) (pp 3–14). New York: Springer.

Thomas, W and Collier, VP. (1997). Two languages are better than one. *Educational Leadership* 55(4): 23–26.

Tuafuti, P. (2010). Additive bilingual education: unlocking the culture of silence. *MAI Review* 1. URL: www.review.mai.ac.nz/index.php/MR/issue/view/15

Vygotsky, LS. (1978). *Mind in Society: The development of higher psychological processes.* Cambridge, MA: Harvard University Press.

Wiederhold, CW and Kagan, S. (2007). *Cooperative Learning & Higher-level Thinking: The Q-matrix* (revised Australian edn). Heatherton, Vic: Hawker Brownlow Education.

Index of figures, tables and exhibits

Figures

Balance learning experiences for production and reception – using VoiceThread (Figure 3.5)	27
Co-construct a SOLO Describe map for describing a monarch butterfly (Figure 4.1)	48
Comparing and contrasting a car and a scooter, based on a plan made with the SOLO Compare and Contrast map in Figure 4.15 (Figure 4.16)	61
Components to balance in teaching English as a second language (Figure 1)	4
Continue to value the use of the first language, particularly if ELLs are literate in L1 (Figure 3.1a and b)	26
Declarative knowledge task and outcome can be at different SOLO levels (Figure 2.2)	14
Describing, explaining and generalising about a kiwifruit, based on a plan made with the SOLO Describe++ map in Figure 4.20 (Figure 4.21)	67
Description of a cultural festival, based on SOLO hexagon plan in Figure 4.6 (Figure 4.7)	50
Description of a lemon, planned with SOLO Describe map (Figure 4.4)	49
Description of the Governor General, planned with SOLO Describe map (Figure 4.5)	49
Display of student work using SOLO hexagons and SOLO vocabulary strips to describe a moment in time (Figure 3.25)	42
ELL's program in Scratch MIT, reinforcing the patterns of sequencing (Figure 4.9)	51
ELLs Skyping with another class to ask questions (Figure 3.23)	41
ELLs using SOLO display strips as prompts for extended abstract responses (Figure 3.11)	30
ELLs work with SOLO display strips and images to sequence events in a cultural festival (Figure 4.13)	56
ELLs write to improve their fluency (Figure 3.6)	27
Know your learner so that you can unleash their passions – ELL shares his learning with the principal (Figure 3.2a and b)	26
Leaderboard tracks student fluency (Figure 3.7)	27
Make learning visible by plotting progress on the Thomas and Collier (1997) chart (Figure 3.3)	26
Make learning visible by plotting progress on the PM reading levels chart (Figure 3.4)	26
Reading with SOLO highlighting – students highlight key vocabulary (Figure 3.12)	30
Sequencing in recount writing, based on a SOLO Sequence map (Figure 4.11)	55
Sequencing with process mapping to show what happened when the fire alarm went off (Figure 4.12)	55
Sequencing writing about a cultural festival with SOLO highlighting (Figure 4.14)	57
SOLO colour-coded display strips with key vocabulary to scaffold writing (Figure 3.10)	30
SOLO Compare and Contrast map a student created using Google Drawings to compare and contrast two dances (Figure 4.17)	62
SOLO hexagons prompt ELLs to use oral language when negotiating the reasons for connecting ideas (Figure 3.24a and b)	42
SOLO self-assessment stickers (Figure 2.3)	15
SOLO stations example – exploring leisure time activities (Figure 2.4)	21–22
Student outcome from SOLO stations – "Why I like Minecraft" by D, aged 6 (Figure 2.5)	23
Student sorts the cut-out paragraphs and then adds key vocabulary (Figure 4.2)	48
Student talks about their learning from writing a description of a titoki tree – ELL aged 7 years (Figure 3.14)	31
Student's construction of extended abstract question, prompted by "See think wonder" routine (Figure 3.22)	40
Student's independent description of a monarch butterfly, with SOLO highlighting (Figure 4.3)	48
Tracking progress in reading with the caterpillar learning log and stickers (Figure 3.20a and b)	35

Using a camera (video or still) to recall the steps in a process (Figure 4.8)	51
Using a full HookED SOLO Describe++ map as a plan for writing a description of a kiwifruit (Figure 4.20)	66
Using a HookED SOLO Describe++ strip in collaborative writing to describe, explain and wonder about a butterfly (Figure 4.19)	66
Using a HookED SOLO Describe++ strip to describe, explain and wonder about an ambulance (Figure 4.18)	66
Using a HOT SOLO Compare and Contrast map to plan to compare and contrast cars and scooters (Figure 4.15)	61
Using food preparation to front-load vocabulary (Figure 3.18)	33
Using images in a sequence sentence frame to describe when Matariki is coming (Figure 4.10)	55
Using pre-recorded language to experience success – Maui and the Sun (YouTube) (Figure 3.15)	32
Using pre-recorded language to experience success – Naughty Cat (Photo Story) (Figure 3.16)	33
Using sentence frames (explicit text structure) and text highlighting (Figure 3.8a and b)	28
Using sentence frames when recording oral language to highlight key vocabulary – Emergent ELL Year 3 talks about a police officer's visit (Figure 3.13a and b)	31
Using SOLO hexagons with colour coding as a SOLO Describe map to plan a description of a cultural festival (Figure 4.6)	49
Using SOLO symbols to indicate a learning task's level of complexity to ELLs (Figure 2.1)	12
Using video to record a speech – student after one year at school (Figure 3.19)	33
Using videos and visuals to front-load vocabulary (Figure 3.17)	33
"What if" questions about leadership to prompt deeper thinking for extended abstract outcomes (Figure 3.21)	39
Writing with SOLO highlighting – key vocabulary when describing an uga (Figure 3.9)	29

Tables

Academic verbs aligned to SOLO levels (Table 2.3)	13
Applications helpful to ELLs in e-learning (Table 3.1)	24
Applying the HookED SOLO Describe++ self-assessment rubric to ELL work that describes, explains and generalises about chopsticks (Table 4.9)	65
Applying the HOT SOLO Compare and Contrast self-assessment rubric to ELL work that compares and contrasts dogs and cats (Table 4.7)	60
Applying the HOT SOLO Describe self-assessment rubric to ELL descriptions (Table 4.2)	47
Applying the HOT SOLO Sequence self-assessment rubric to ELL sequencing work (Table 4.4)	54
Different labels, similar stages in acquiring L2 (Table 2.1)	11
A guide to the SOLO L2 lesson plan (Table 2.9)	19–20
Key ways of knowing your ELLs (Table 3.2)	25
Provide opportunities to learn from shared events – ELL writes on the Newmarket School Fiesta (Table 3.3)	26
Question types classified by SOLO level (Table 3.8)	38
Self-assessment rubric for declarative knowledge, built using levels in SOLO Taxonomy (Table 1.3)	8
Self-assessment rubric for functioning knowledge, built using levels in SOLO Taxonomy (Table 1.2)	7
Sequencing events in a cultural festival in response to prompts at each SOLO level (Table 4.5)	56
SOLO-differentiated questioning framework for three levels of cognitive complexity (Table 3.9)	38
SOLO declarative knowledge rubric for ELL language functions in explaining causes (Table 2.7)	17
SOLO declarative knowledge levels and ELL responses (Table 2.2)	12
SOLO declarative knowledge rubric for answering subjective questions using a sentence claim (Table 3.6)	34
SOLO functioning knowledge rubric for different levels of L2 acquisition (Table 2.6)	16
SOLO functioning knowledge rubric for trying to answer subjective questions using a sentence claim (Table 3.5)	34
SOLO functioning knowledge rubric for willingness to communicate in English L2 with others (Table 2.5)	15
SOLO levels, symbols, hand signs and academic verbs (Table 1.1)	6

Supporting language structures for a compare and contrast task (Table 4.6)	57
Supporting language structures for a describing task (Table 4.1)	46
Supporting language structures for a sequencing task (Table 4.3)	51
Supporting language structures for describing, explaining and generalising (Table 4.8)	62
Using SOLO and constructive alignment to plan learning experiences and assessment – an example (Table 2.8)	18
Using SOLO levels to write a reflection on the written description in Figure 3.14 (Table 3.4)	32
Using SOLO to differentiate goals in a listening activity with PM readers (Table 3.7)	36
Using the SOLO-differentiated questioning framework to plan questions across all stages of L2 acquisition (Table 3.10)	39
Zone of proximal development and L2 acquisition (Table 2.4)	14

Exhibits

Caterpillar learning log for tracking progress in reading (Exhibit 3.1)	35
Chart for monitoring the SOLO level of questions asked (Exhibit 3.2)	40
Checklist of questions when planning for academic achievement in L2 learning (Exhibit 1.1)	8
HookED SOLO Describe++ map (Exhibit 4.7)	63
HookED SOLO Describe++ strip (Exhibit 4.8)	64
HookED SOLO Describe++ self-assessment rubric (Exhibit 4.9)	64
HookED SOLO hexagons rubric (Exhibit 3.3)	43
HOT SOLO Compare and Contrast map as a relational supporting strategy (Exhibit 4.5)	58
HOT SOLO Compare and Contrast self-assessment rubric for SOLO-differentiated outcomes (Exhibit 4.6)	59
HOT SOLO Describe map as a multistructural supporting strategy (Exhibit 4.1)	45
HOT SOLO Describe self-assessment rubric for SOLO-differentiated outcomes (Exhibit 4.2)	46
HOT SOLO Sequence map as a relational supporting strategy (Exhibit 4.3)	52
HOT SOLO Sequence self-assessment rubric for SOLO-differentiated outcomes (Exhibit 4.4)	53

www.ingramcontent.com/pod-product-compliance
Lightning Source LLC
Chambersburg PA
CBHW080046230426
43672CB00014B/2831